How to Help your **Autistic Spectrum** Child

How to Help your **Autistic Spectrum** Child

Practical ways to make family
life run more smoothly

Jackie Brealy and Beverly Davies

white
LADDER

Important note

'Autism spectrum disorder' is a title that covers the conditions known as autism and Asperger syndrome, generally referred to as ASD within the book.

All the information is given in good faith; it is given for general use and should not be seen as applicable to any individual situation. Anyone seeking advice on health should see their GP or appropriate health professional in the first instance.

How to help your autistic spectrum child: Practical ways to make family life run more smoothly

This second edition published in 2015 by White Ladder Press, an imprint of Crimson Publishing Ltd, 19–21c Charles Street, Bath BA1 1HX.

First edition published by White Ladder Press in 2007.

© Crimson Publishing 2015

The rights of Jackie Brealy and Beverly Davies to be identified as the authors of this work have been asserted by them in accordance with the Copyright, Designs and Patents Act 1988.

British Library Cataloguing in Publication Data
A catalogue record for this book is available from the British Library.

ISBN 978 1 90828 198 2

Typeset by IDSUK (DataConnection) Ltd
Printed and bound in Great Britain by TJ International Ltd, Padstow, Cornwall

We would like to dedicate this book to Matt, who has grown up into a fine and caring young man and encouraged us to share his story with you, and also to his wonderful brother Paul, who was a guide and an example to him and remains so to this day.

Contents

About the authors

Jackie

The idea for this book first germinated because, in the initial shock after my son Matt's diagnosis with autism, I was looking for a book that would help me with practical ideas, and I couldn't find one. As time went by I evolved lots of practical tips of my own, which I wanted to share. I studied for an NVQ Level 3 in special needs, worked in special needs schooling and with individual children, as well as living with ASD at home with Matt, so I understand from both sides how to help these children and their families. I realised that what I was doing was really helping Matt and other children I worked with, and wanted to pass the information on. As luck would have it, the parents of one of these children were publishers and asked if I would like to write a book about what I do. I must admit that this scared me, but I was lucky to be partnered up with Beverly Davies, a writer. So I empty out the contents of my head and, voila, Bev turns it into a book. We both hope you will find it helpful.

Beverly

I have been a journalist for many years, specialising in health and family issues. Putting together this book has given me a keen interest in how we help children with special educational needs, and an awareness of the huge problems that beset parents, not least in finding the right school for their child. What started as a straightforward writing job has led me to become a volunteer reading helper in a primary school. It has also led to a real friendship with a very inspiring person. Jackie is a brave and compassionate woman who knows that problems, however terrible, are there to be dealt with, and has an instinctive grasp of practical solutions. She has a massive optimism, and a belief that everyone should have a chance to be the best they can. This translates into a body of good advice, and a conviction that most situations can, at the very least, be made better.

Introduction
to the second edition

When we got together to write the first edition of this book, back in 2005, discovering that your child was on the autistic spectrum was, for many parents, the start of a journey into the unknown. Our book was designed to be resolutely practical, and we hoped it would be a lifeline for families who were having a difficult time of it. We are more than happy that this has proved to be the case, and that as we embark on this comprehensively updated edition quite a lot has changed.

Books such as the bestseller *The Curious Incident of the Dog in the Night-time*, television programmes and feature articles have helped to raise general awareness of the autistic spectrum. However, awareness is one thing; understanding and tolerance are quite another. Life can still be very difficult for families with a member on the autistic spectrum, and that is where the advice in this book, reconfigured for a new generation, comes in.

It is probably safe to say that there is more acceptance of 'difference' than there was when we started; more research, more investigation and lots of promising new findings – such as new research that shows that autistic people have more brain connections than is the norm and studies that suggest that, in some cases, autism is outgrown as a child gets older.

But does that translate into an easier life for families with a member on the autistic spectrum? The jury is still out on that one.

We wrote the first edition of this book when my autistic son Matthew was 14 years old. The book included my front-line experience of bringing up a child with autism and my strategies and tips. Matt is now 24, and in this second edition, I am able to draw upon another decade of experience and share with you how far he, and we, have come.

When I look at Matt, who has been sharing a flat with friends and working as a painter and decorator, I am amazed and thankful for how far we have come. As a family we have been through some terrible times, the worst of which was the loss of Matt's big brother, Paul, who was killed in a car crash. This book still contains a lot of references to Paul, as he continues to be a beloved part of our family.

In this new edition of our book we will cover my family's own hard-won tips to help your ASD child deal with grief and bereavement, and some surprising things that we found out ourselves along the way. Interestingly, this is one of those situations where the ASD mindset can be a positive advantage.

I feel that a lot of Matt's achievements as a young adult are a direct result of the way that we brought him up, so all my advice for dealing with your ASD child at different ages and stages is still here, as well as a wealth of new hints to take you through the teenage years and beyond.

We've also included some other children's stories in this new edition, showing you how other parents have dealt with the issues that having an ASD child brings, and how they have coped.

We have all come a long way – but it is important not to forget how and why it all began.

Introduction to the first edition

Getting a diagnosis of autism spectrum disorder is not the end of the world – but it is the beginning of a journey.

A boy is standing at the side of the road. He is screaming and crying and flapping his arms, in a state bordering on complete panic. To an outsider it looks as if he is having a terrible tantrum, but I know there is much more to it than that. His unhappiness is hard to bear. I don't know what to do about it and, of more immediate importance, I don't know how to get him across the road.

Because Matt was my third child I knew there was something different about him from day one. He didn't connect, he didn't make eye contact, he didn't walk until he was two and his speech development was very slow. The diagnosis of Asperger syndrome was a long time coming. In fact, when we finally knew what was wrong, it was almost a relief to be able to give Matt's problems a name and to feel that we had some idea of what to expect.

Now Matt is 14. He goes to regular school, and a casual observer, seeing him with his friends, would probably think he was a teenager like any other. He is in a band at school, mucks around and gets into a bit of trouble from time to time, just like the rest of the boys. He communicates with other people reasonably well and has pretty good social skills.

The normal teenager and the autistic teenager in Matt are slightly at loggerheads. He wants to be like everybody else, but he doesn't really know where to draw the line, so he gets into more trouble than the others. He will still sometimes do extreme things – he walked through a bonfire because he wanted to see what it was like (his shoes melted, so I like to think he wouldn't do it again, though of course I cannot rule it out). He still needs routine and likes to know exactly what is happening and when.

It has been a long journey from that terrible day at the side of the road to where we are now, and I want to tell you how we made it.

If you have just had a diagnosis of autism spectrum disorder (ASD) for your child, don't panic. I just want everyone to know that however bleak the diagnosis can seem, you may well be able to make the sort of progress that we have made with Matt. I don't want to paint a picture that is too rosy, but I have as much pride and joy in Matt as I do in my other children. I think over time, partly because I am now trained in learning support for special needs pupils, partly because I have a habit of observing and analysing behaviour, I have found some good ways of dealing with Matt and his problems, and I would like to share them with you.

It took a long time to get to the bottom of those roadside panics of Matt's, but I got there in the end. At first I didn't understand his anxiety, I thought he was just having a terrible tantrum. I used to pick him up and put him back in his buggy and carry on, even though he was screaming at me. It wasn't until I started to look at just when he was doing it that I realised that there was a pattern. If we were trying to cross the road he would get in a total state and curl up on the pavement, screaming. He would start flapping his arms and would get really panicky. His anxiety went off the scale. I just couldn't say or do anything to control him. He would keep repeating the word 'cars' because he couldn't talk very well at that time. After a while, I understood. He was getting into a state because the cars were coming in too many different directions for him to concentrate on them all.

I needed an idea to help him with crossing the road, so at home we set up his car mat with cars and played at crossing the road using the toy cars so that we could check which side they would come from when you were crossing. Then when we went out we could put into practice which way you would have to look to see the cars coming.

A lot of parents get stuck into the trap of trying to make their child behave in a 'normal' way, rather than trying to understand what the problems are. I always try to be responsive to Matt's problems, just as I was with the cars, and I don't try to make him behave the way my other children behaved. In fact, that would be impossible, because he is so fundamentally different.

Some parents may well think that their child will get over or grow out of these things or that they can simply force him to change, without ever realising that there are reasons for a lot of the strange behaviour or understanding the implacable if bizarre logic behind it. They don't work out how to help their child to cope with whatever is upsetting him.

When we are bringing up our children there are a lot of things that we simply never explain because we assume that they somehow automatically know them, but they may puzzle away at something for ages and worry about it without our realising. We need to see things through children's eyes. Bringing up Matt made me realise that you should never assume they know or understand something. I have to go right back to basics and explain things every time; he can't just accept what I am saying.

With my other children I think I was a run-of-the-mill parent. I can see how I have changed with Matt because he is so different. I often think I should have explained things more to the older two. The experience I have had with Matt has taught me a lot, which I try to relay to other parents through my work, when we talk about the children's worries and try to find a way around them.

Once you know it is an autism spectrum disorder

- Don't panic. Most situations can be improved.
- Try to look at things through your child's eyes.
- Try to understand your child. If you realise *why* they do things you will begin to see how you can help.
- See what your child does in troublesome situations and write it down. It is likely that a pattern will start to emerge.
- Be prepared to go over things with them time and time again.
- Love your child for who they are, and help them to be proud of themselves; don't try and change them – but do try to do something about things that cause them problems.
- Take a look at every source of help and advice that comes your way. The more support you can get the better – and that's what this book is for.

1

Defining the condition

Autism is a complex developmental disability that affects the way children communicate and relate to the world around them. The spectrum of autism means that children are affected by the condition to different degrees. According to figures from the National Autistic Society around 700,000 people, or more than one in 100 of the population, are somewhere on the spectrum, which ranges from severe autism, through high-functioning autism to Asperger syndrome at the more able end.

If you suspect that your child's behaviour puts them somewhere on the spectrum you may still find that a definitive diagnosis is a long time coming. Autistic difficulties are usually present from birth, though children may appear to develop normally until about age two to three before problems become hard to ignore. In the past, many people could not get a diagnosis until their child started school or even later. Now things have improved in this area to the extent that diagnosis – and helpful treatments – can kick in at a much younger age. Although ASDs are not curable, they respond to treatment, especially if this starts as early as possible. If you feel that your child may be affected it is worth pressing for a specialist diagnosis as soon as possible, making your GP your first port of call.

You can see why it can be hard to spot ASDs in very young children. Diagnosis is based on observing behaviour; after all this is a handicap that is social rather than physical. You can only really spot problems with social interaction when a child reaches toddler age, although parents are often sure that there is something amiss from very early on.

Common things to look out for

Although this is a condition that needs to be diagnosed on a very individual basis, rendering a tick-box list of symptoms unhelpful, there are some factors that will help to point you towards a diagnosis. ASDs affect the way an individual relates to others and communicates with them, disrupting the development of social, communication and cognitive skills. Common factors for both autism and Asperger syndrome are:

Difficulty in communicating

- problems in understanding language – very literal interpretation with no appreciation of nuance
- problems in using language – if verbal, speech patterns are often peculiar
- problems in recognising or interpreting facial expressions, gestures and tone of voice

Difficulty in social relationships

- can seem aloof and indifferent to people
- lack of two-way social relationships
- lack of empathy/sympathy – find it hard to understand that others may see things from a different viewpoint
- sometimes want to establish a relationship but no idea how to

Lack of imagination and creative play

- fear of change, preference for sameness – restricted interests: limited play

Together, these three areas of difficulty are known as the **triad of impairments**. This triad is often accompanied by a narrow and repetitive pattern of activity that is comforting to the child.

It is important to consider what the triad means to each individual child: the areas of difficulty may not be equally impaired, and the results of impairment may be different at different stages of development, so treatment should always be tailored to the individual.

Children with ASDs find it hard to make sense of what is going on around them. Understanding other people's expressions of emotion can be difficult or impossible for them and it can be very hard to develop friendships. The difficulty people with ASDs have in imagining what someone else may be thinking or feeling is explained by the idea that they lack what is known as a 'theory of mind'. A child with autism may well think that you know everything that they know or think, and it will not occur to them to try to communicate any of it to you.

The need for routine is paramount. When a child has trouble comprehending their environment and no way of predicting what will happen next, then routine is a great source of comfort and safety. Any attempt to vary a routine or pattern may lead to challenging behaviour from the child. However, on the bright side, this dependence on routine and structure can be a positive thing in a classroom context.

Children with Asperger syndrome are not as withdrawn as classic autists; they often enjoy contact and want to be sociable, though their difficulty in 'reading' social signals from other people can make this hard for them. While people with Asperger syndrome often speak fluently, they may not take much notice of the reaction of listeners. These children do not necessarily have any of the accompanying learning disabilities associated with autism, and will often enter mainstream school. They can be very good at learning facts and figures, though they do find it hard to think in abstract ways. The idea of the autistic genius is something of a modern myth. In fact, ASD IQs go right across the range from genius to severe learning difficulty, and up to 75% of people with ASDs have learning difficulties of some kind.

Clarifying ASD

ASD is:

- a developmental disorder
- associated with unusual response to sensory stimulation
- four times more likely to occur in boys than girls
- found in all social groups.

ASD may be:

- genetically linked – you may find other family members with ASD
- accompanied by epilepsy and other disorders such as ADD (attention deficit disorder) and OCD (obsessive compulsive disorder)
- accompanied by particular skills such as music, drawing or maths
- accompanied by moderate or severe learning difficulties.

ASD is not:

- caused by parental rejection
- caused by stress, though stress and anxiety may make the symptoms worse.

How we got our diagnosis

Because Matt was my third child, I knew from very early on that he was not exactly standard issue. I'm not at all sure that I would have picked things up so quickly if he had been my first. Despite my early worries, it took a long time to get a diagnosis; in fact he was nearly eight when we knew for sure.

Apparently autistic children are often late developers, and Matt certainly bore that out. At 18 months he wasn't talking or walking or doing other age-appropriate things. I brought my concerns up with the health visitor but didn't really get anywhere. When Matt was two and a half I went back, and they still said I had to wait until he was a bit older. When he started nursery, still in nappies, they noticed that he was a loner who always played by himself and had no interest in getting to know the other children. The staff found it very hard to get any response from him; he seemed to have no comprehension of what was going on around him.

We had a huge daily battle to get anywhere when Matt was a toddler. He used to flap his hands and get upset in a way that children usually don't, getting very angry about things when they didn't seem to make sense to him. We thought a lot of his temper was because he was frustrated that he couldn't walk yet. When he did start walking he fell over a lot, and some of his behaviour was downright disturbing. If we had someone around to visit he would scream all the time. We couldn't sit and chat or have tea, because he would just scream. In consequence, we didn't have people around, or go out much, because it was such a hassle.

Things certainly didn't seem right with Matt, but we didn't know what was wrong. We just thought it was extreme quirky-toddler behaviour – we thought his toddler stage was going to last forever. Just to go and do the shopping was a nightmare. Getting him dressed was a daily struggle, and the other children were always put on hold. It seemed really wrong.

When I went to the GP my main concern was that Matt never responded to me. I had thought that his hearing might be at the root of it, but that proved to be fine. Then I mentioned his lack of responsiveness, at which stage we were referred to a paediatrician who did the test for epilepsy and sent us on to a child psychologist, who took a history of everything that had happened to Matt from birth onwards.

The tests revealed both epilepsy and Asperger syndrome. Although I had heard of autism, Asperger was a completely unknown quantity. When we first got the diagnosis, we were dumbfounded. We didn't know what we needed to do. It took us months to come to terms with it. A disability you can see is much easier to accept than a mental disability. Every time we looked at Matt we couldn't believe what we had been told. He looked so normal and he was such a sweet child in so many ways that I found it very hard to believe that something had gone wrong with his brain.

A lot of parents are reluctant to take their children in to be assessed because they are afraid of that label, and I can understand that. But the label opens up a world for these children to get much more of the help they need, for them to understand why they feel so different from everyone else, and for you, as a parent, to understand them. At the mild end of the spectrum, without a diagnosis it would be possible for an autistic person to go their whole life without knowing why they felt different. If you are older when you find out what is causing your problems, you can start to deal with your condition, and, if you so wish, to break some of the habits that make you look different in society. As an individual, fitting in can help you if you want to be in the group. We all have to modify our behaviour to some extent. As the parent of a child with an ASD, you have to make some of these decisions for them.

I believe that getting the label is better than not knowing, and it has certainly helped with Matt. Some parents give their children all the details of the condition. I didn't choose to do that with Matt. I felt that showing him everything on a list of behaviour would make him think 'Well, I have to do this because it is part of my condition, and I can't do that because that is part of my condition.' A list like that is both limiting and defining.

However, I am really glad that we got Matt's diagnosis sorted out when he was young. If we hadn't known until later, it would have been much harder because there would have been different barriers. It is important to get a diagnosis for practical reasons, too. Diagnosis in our case led to statementing and, with any luck, should lead to a proper consideration of your child's educational needs. The label may qualify you for Disability Living Allowance or a disabled parking permit, which can certainly make life easier. Really, anything that helps has got to be worth it.

I never want to change Matt – as he once said to me, 'Who is different, me or you?' – and he has every right to be the person he is.

Spotting the signs

Recognition of ASD has increased since I was first looking for answers with Matt. Early diagnosis helps in so many ways. There are lots of things that can be done to help your child, and the sooner you start, the more likely they are to be effective. It can certainly help to get started before behaviour patterns get too entrenched.

If this is your first child you have no point of comparison, so there are things you could easily miss and your worries may only become clear over time. With the late emergence of all the signs, and average gaps between children of two to three years, it is quite likely that by the time you realise that something is seriously amiss with your first child you will either have or be expecting your second.

It is not always easy to get an early diagnosis however sure you are that there is something wrong. We saw five or six people before the diagnosis, and the extent of Matt's problems emerged only gradually. If you notice that your child is a loner, or doesn't make eye contact, or talk, or point at anything when they might be expected to, you might want to look for other things in their behaviour that chime with this diagnosis. There are not many absolute rules, however. Most children with ASD don't want to share information or point out things. Matt would take my hand and lead me to what he wanted me to see, but that is far from typical; he was always unusually communicative for an ASD child. If you are worried, make a list of your concerns and take them to your GP. See Chapter 15 for more on getting help from health professionals.

If your child is very young, you might first mention your worries to your health visitor. Seeing your GP is likely to be the next stage, and you should then be referred for a formal assessment, ideally by a team of professionals including a specialist psychologist and perhaps a speech and language therapist. If your child is school age, you might want to make an initial appointment with the school's special educational needs co-ordinator (SENCO) to talk over your worries. In any case, formal assessment should be followed by a written diagnostic report and recommendations.

A word about CHAT

CHAT stands for Checklist of Autism in Toddlers and is a screening tool developed at Cambridge University's Autism Research Centre. It consists of a series of simple, but defining questions for parents and GP, such as whether the child points at things to show interest in them, enjoys pretend play or takes an interest in other children. The researchers suggest that it should be included in the GP's 18-month check of all toddlers. This does not happen at present but, if you have concerns, you could ask your GP to do the test. Details can be found on the National Autistic Society website (www.autism.org.uk) or the website for Child Autism UK (formerly known as Peach), an early years autism charity which supports parents and specialises in behavioural interventions for children (www.childautism.org.uk). With an eye to the effectiveness of early intervention, it is worth pressing for a diagnosis if you have worries, and, while not in itself a diagnosis, the CHAT test is a substantial first step.

What if you have trouble getting a diagnosis?

A written diagnosis, where a health professional writes that your child has an autism spectrum disorder, is essential if you and your child are to get the help and support you need.

But it can be dreadful for parents who know something is wrong, suspect it is ASD and cannot convince health professionals. This can be a very isolating experience and, alas, is not uncommon. If you are having trouble getting a diagnosis, there are some steps you can take.

- Find out the way through the maze from support groups (the National Autistic Society could be your first port of call) and fellow parents.
- Try to work with the professionals and avoid conflict, even if you disagree. Give a clear summary of your child's problems. Some professionals are against 'labelling' children, but the 'label' given by a clear diagnosis is the only way to get the help they need.
- Make sure you feel happy that you have a complete diagnosis. Remember that ASD goes right across the spectrum of intelligence – so a child's intelligence levels have nothing to do with whether or not they are on the ASD spectrum. Many other disorders such as OCD, ADD or challenging behaviour can be a part of the ASD, so if you feel you have not received a complete diagnosis, keep going.
- Accept that it can take time – a lot of time – to get the clear diagnosis you need. You have to trust your instincts as a parent – you know your child better than anyone.

The Elizabeth Newson Centre in Nottingham helps parents of children with developmental communication disorders to obtain a specialist diagnostic assessment of their child as early as possible. The centre is a charity and parents can make a direct referral, although for funding purposes it is probably best to be referred by your GP or paediatrician. (01623 490879; www.autismeastmidlands.org.uk).

Dealing with the triad

There is only so much you can do here. You are dealing with a person and you can't make parts of their personality go away, but there are things you can try that may help in almost every area.

- **Difficulty understanding language** – use one of the specially developed communication systems (PECS for straightforward communication, Makaton where things are more severe – details in Chapter 2), also CDs, and, if your child likes TV, use DVDs to help you, or even make your own little films. You could make a short film on aspects of daily life, like dressing, or eating at the table or introducing members of the family over and over again until the child starts to recognise them.
- **Difficulty showing or understanding emotions** – when they smile, say 'That's a lovely happy face', when they cry, say 'You are so sad', underlining the emotion they are feeling. Get them to draw someone's happy face, so they associate the feeling with a person.

- **Difficulty with social interaction** – if they are cut off, encourage them to socialise. This would not work for children who are really isolated in their autism. With such children I would see if I could find something they liked so that I could get a connection going. Sit nearby, playing with something they might find interesting, and let them come to you.
- **Difficulty with two-way social relationships** – ask them for more information, and more and more. In the end it will have to become a dialogue. For turn-taking, play games with a couple of children and say 'Jackie's go', 'Michael's go', 'Soon your go, Fred, wait for your turn', and repeat endlessly until, with luck, the penny drops.
- **Lack of empathy** – they won't understand how their words can make people feel. Say similar things back to them: 'You look spotty', 'Why is your hair a mess?' and try to get them to see that it is not very nice to be on the receiving end of such comments. Get a 'feelings' book that contains pictures of people showing various different emotions in different situations.
- **No idea how to form friendships** – teach them to go up to someone and say 'Can I play?' If they start doing this at a young age, they will not be so self-conscious.
- **Lack of imagination** – show a picture then prod them to think about it with questions, such as 'Do you think the child in the picture is happy or sad?' so you are getting them to use some imagination and make up a story.
- **Fear of change** – change is a part of life, and I think ASD children have to learn to accept it. Don't entirely protect them from it, but be supportive if it causes problems, and put strategies in place to make it easier to cope with.
- **Restricted interests/limited play** – ASD children are likely to have their obsessions, and not want to look beyond them for play. Offer them something extra to play with: expand one game with extra components.
- **Need for routine and repetition** – if this is not causing a family problem it is probably best to go along with your child's rituals as much as possible. For help when it does become a problem, see Chapter 8.
- **Difficulties with co-ordination** – Some ASD children have difficulties with co-ordination. You can try things like wooden puzzles, or getting them to put icing on biscuits as fun ways of improving hand-eye co-ordination. Another great idea is a dance mat with a screen game by which you improve co-ordination by stepping on the right colours. This can also help with spatial awareness.

Sensory sensitivities

A child with ASD may well have fears and phobias to do with noise, light, touch and smell, though hopefully not all of these at once. These fears will have an impact on their behaviour and may well make them reluctant to go into some places or situations. As they are highly unlikely to be able to verbalise this reluctance, what you will get is a terrified and possibly angry child making a scene. As with so many of these issues, understanding their fears and finding ways to come to terms with them, or simply avoiding difficult situations, is the key.

- For instance, your child might not want to get into the car because of the **smell** of the air freshener. You could simply take it down, or you could talk to them about smells, and how they feel about smells. You could take them to the shop and get them to choose a freshener to put in the car, and then ask them to put it in the car. This will give them a feeling of being in control of something that they find difficult.
- As you learn what smells they don't like, you will know what could trigger problems in shops, other people's homes or at school. Here, the dining room and science lab can be particular sources of anxiety, and if there are likely to be problems, you could ask the school whether you and your child can go round the relevant rooms together to see what they dislike. Talking about these problems in advance may well defuse the fear for your child when they have a lesson there.
- You can use the same tips for **touch**: find out what they don't like the feel of and why. Play with some of these things. It will help if you touch whatever it is first so that your child sees you having fun with it. Don't let it touch them until they are ready. They may never come to like the thing, but seeing you play with it will help them to see it in a less threatening way.
- **Noise** can really hurt and upset them. It is important to find out what they don't like, as it will crop up all the time. Encourage them to play music quietly on an iPod, so that they can control the volume and, with any luck, find things that they enjoy. When they are old enough let them use earplugs, under your supervision, to cut down on noise that they find upsetting.
- **Light** can cause problems and, if this is the case, get them some sunglasses and sit them away from sunny windows.

2

The importance of starting early

In the bad old days, when it was unusual to get a diagnosis of autism at a young age, many opportunities to help and understand ASD children were lost. Even now, although diagnosis may come by around age two, this is not always the case.

Early intervention, however, is very much to be hoped for: it can reduce the build-up of behavioural problems and stop some habits from becoming too entrenched. As the difficulties of the triad relate to every aspect of a child's life, so across-the-board parental involvement is paramount. Useful techniques for dealing with your child, such as the ones I am going to suggest in this chapter, can be incorporated into family life as early as possible, and there are some very helpful programmes that parents can get involved in. Start as soon as you can with the ideas below, so that family life can be easier and more peaceful for everyone involved.

Learning with pictures

When Matt was small, I started using pictures that were relevant to him to help. I didn't know it then, but this is a standard treatment. At the time it was just a system I evolved because I had to find a way for Matt to understand me more quickly, as my two older children needed me too. He responded to the pictures, which really helped. Then he started mimicking me and, eventually, his verbal skills became fantastic. But when he was little, if he became cross, he would revert to the pictures. I had little round disc pictures of happy, sad, angry and worried faces on the fridge for him, to help him express emotions when he couldn't find the words. If he put up the angry face picture then he could have time out in his bedroom, and he was grateful then that I knew what he needed, even though he couldn't quite express it for himself.

Initially, to help him with getting dressed, I used photographs of his actual clothes stuck onto the drawers they were in, so that he could see at a glance where they were. I started that when he was two and kept it going until he was about eight, when he finally clicked that things were always in the same drawer. The dressing routine involved me telling him the things to put on in order as I went to and fro past his room in the morning, and gradually, over time, he got his own routine going.

Difficulty with social communication is a key factor in ASD, and one way of addressing it is through the use of picture symbols. Children with ASD tend to be visual learners, so pictures can help them make sense of the world. Photographs, line drawings, objects and written words can be helpful ways to accompany and augment speech but, as in so many areas, ASD makes communication more complicated. Children with ASD may find a line drawing less confusing than a photo. They may register details more strongly than the whole thing, and so can be confused if a photo used does not correspond exactly with the object that it symbolises. For instance, they will see that a line drawing of 'crisps' relates to all crisps, where they can't see that a picture of a particular brand has anything at all in common with any other crisps.

PECS (The Picture Exchange Communication System)

PECS was developed to help young children with autism to learn how to initiate requests and communicate what they need. They have to learn how communication works, which is hard for them. The basic understanding that another person may not know what you want until you tell them is missing in their make-up, so they do not intrinsically understand the need to communicate. For example, an ASD boy who is thirsty assumes his mother knows that he wants a drink. If, knowing he is thirsty, she hasn't produced a drink, there is no point in asking her for one. Children can learn how communication works if they are taught to exchange a symbol for something they want. PECS has proved to be very effective, it is easy to use and involves no expensive equipment, testing or training, though professionals and parents can take training courses.

The earlier the children start PECS, the better. You will communicate more quickly with them and will have less anxiety to deal with as, from an early age, children who have mastered it will be used to being able to tell you what they want.

First, associate the picture symbol with the actual thing it represents by attaching a paper symbol to the object (e.g. 'biscuit'). When the child has started to associate the symbol with the real thing, then an identical symbol a little away from the actual thing lets the parent or carer show the symbol while telling the child what to get. Symbols should be used first with things that motivate the child, such as 'biscuit', or 'drink', and the rate at which they can be introduced varies from child to child.

By establishing the individual's likes among food and toys, the child is taught in a step-by-step process to exchange a symbol for the item he or she wants. There are six carefully structured stages of PECS.

1. The child learns the picture exchange.
2. The child actively finds someone to give a symbol to as a request.
3. The child discriminates between several symbols.
4. The child uses a portable communication book containing picture symbols.
5. The child constructs simple sentences, both requests and comments.
6. The child gradually achieves independence from the helper's prompts and learns that communication is a two-way process which gets the desired results.

PECS often helps in the development of spoken words and encourages interaction, and possibly eye contact, as the children have to find someone to give the symbol to. Children learn to communicate using PECS because they are motivated to get something they want. With severely autistic children who cannot communicate verbally, all they use is their PECS book. For my ASD students I get a small diary and put in a sheet to which I attach all the pictures that describe their day at school. If the children want to communicate something, they learn to use the PECS picture of a drink if they want a drink, and so on, and if they want to tell you something, they show you in the book. The picture symbols can help make their environment predictable and organised, which helps them keep calm.

lunchtime   **now**

Parents should persevere for ages with PECS. It takes the children a long time to realise what the cards are for, so you have to plug away for as much as a year, but then you have opened up a channel of communication that is invaluable. You have to make sure that the pictures they have do mean something to them; some autistic children may not relate to stick figures, for instance, so you need to personalise the PECS system to your child.

Further information about PECS can be obtained from Pyramid Educational Consultants UK Ltd (01273 609555; www.pecs-unitedkingdom.com). For a fee, they can send a consultant for a home visit to get you started.

Choices and changes

Picture symbols can be very useful when introducing the idea of choices, such as different foods or play activities. Here the benefit can be encouraging the children to think about trying an available activity that they may enjoy, rather than sticking to one repetitive activity or remaining passive.

Another useful tool is a 'changes' card, which shows them that what they were expecting to do has changed. This card is a question mark (?), and becomes very familiar, which helps them to be less anxious about changes in their daily schedule that would otherwise make them very concerned; it works right across the spectrum – even quite severely autistic children come to recognise it.

Expressing anxiety

Again, when feelings boil over, a visual method is often the best way to express it. Have a big drawing of a thermometer somewhere in the house with zero at the bottom and numbers going up to ten at the top. Children can point out how angry they are feeling – and sometimes this is much better than putting it into words. When they show you that their anger is starting to build up, you can do something about it straight away.

Learning through play

It is always worth making the time to play with your ASD child, they will learn such a lot from it. With severely autistic children you already know they don't want physical contact. Matt's case was milder, but when he was young he would offer me just a part of him to hug – he would never hurl himself into my arms like a normal toddler. He became quite cuddly – we taught him to be, partly through the example of his big brothers, partly through play.

I have endlessly played games where I have said things like 'I am going to cuddle dolly and it will make him feel better because dolly is feeling sad, now.' This helped Matt to learn emotions that he didn't really feel for himself. For instance, one day when I cut myself in the kitchen he said, 'You must need a cuddle because you have hurt yourself', but he would not have felt that for himself. He learned to come and give spontaneous hugs and say, 'I love you.' When he was younger it was clearly something learned, that he felt was the right thing to say or do, but later he meant it. Some ASD children really don't understand the concept of love, they have to learn it. Others may not be able to say it but when you look at them, their eyes show liking or love even if they can't express it.

Parents can help them discover feelings and imagination and emotions through play – 'The dolly is sad'; 'The dolly is happy'; 'I love the dolly'. Keep going with all this for years and it pays off: in the end it may become what they mean, not what they have learned. I think this could work with quite severely autistic children, too. They do tend to shut themselves away, but you can, while remaining respectful of their condition, try to get through to them with play. You have to allow that they can't always cope with contact and will always need time out from it, but if you can touch them for a few minutes a day, you achieve something.

One child I worked with wouldn't make eye contact at all, she would always look down at my feet, so I made some cut-out paper eyes and stuck them on my feet. She looked at the eyes there for a while, and then I slowly moved them up my body over a period of six months or so until they ended up on my forehead, then I took them away and she looked at my real eyes. I knew that I had made contact. Then we made up a game where I would say 'Look at my eyes' and we would play eye-rolling games. This took away her fear of eye contact.

<hr>

Toy story

Set up by Lesley Burton, who was amazed that she couldn't find a shop or mail order catalogue selling the kind of toys she wanted for her autistic son, Eddie, the SenseToys website (www.sensetoys.com) features colourful, fun toys and lots of inspiring ideas for how to play with them with your special needs child.

The toys are carefully chosen to appeal to children with special educational needs – there are lots of play tips and explanations of why each toy meets specific needs. It is truly a family business – each month Eddie's Choice, a favourite toy, is offered at a special price. Lesley says,

'I set up the website because I wanted to let people know what was out there. It is all very well having special toys but if you don't know what to do with them, or how to engage your child, it is not much use. It is not the toy, it is what you do with it that gives it value for an autistic child. The website is full of play ideas that people seem to find very helpful. It encourages parents to know they are not the only ones whose child is throwing things over his head and not seeming interested in anything.'

<hr>

Programmes and schemes to help ASD children

Applied Behaviour Analysis – the Lovaas Programme

This form of behavioural therapy is based on more than 30 years of clinical experience and research carried out by Dr O. Ivar Lovaas in the USA and has been available for some 25 years in this country. It is ideally an early intervention programme for children with ASD, and operates as an intensive home-based regime, targeting the learning of skills broken down into small, achievable steps, taught in a very structured way with a lot of praise and reinforcement. It focuses on one-to-one teaching undertaken by sets of tutors, and takes one thing at a time, concentrating on and repeating it until the child is seen to have truly learned it. It is very individual; learning blocks as simple as pointing to something or clapping hands are chosen for each child, and every small success is rewarded.

Anne Smith is an ABA therapist and has seen the benefits the programme can bring to parents as well as children. 'The programme is good for parents, not least because every day when they wake up it gives them targets. In a situation where maybe a child seems isolated from the family all the time, life can seem terrifyingly without structure. This gives a structure. If they have a goal – to teach the child to clap his hands or put one brick on top of another – at least for part of the day they have something to work on which is for the benefit of their child. The programme can be quite a challenge for parents. The hours are long – as much as 40 hours a week – and the house is full of people all the time.

'I get so much enjoyment from the work. I love the children, and the reward, when you get them to make a pile of bricks or whatever, is enormous. Finding the things to do for some of them is very, very hard, because they don't like toys or playing, but there is always something; whether they like being tickled, thrown in the air or watching twinkling lights. Whatever it is you can find it by watching them and then slowly, when they are comfortable with you, you can get them to do some little thing, whether it is take a crisp or clap their hands and you can build up from there. Some of them never get beyond the early stages. I had one little boy who after three years still couldn't say anything, though he could do every puzzle under the sun, was toilet-trained and could go to the shops with his mother. There are so many ways of measuring success.

'There is no such thing as a "cure"; what we hope we are doing is helping to make things easier. I feel very privileged that I have had the opportunity to be involved and to see these children for the wonderful kids they are. They all have something special. There is this terrible myth of these sad children and nearly all the ones I have worked with have had a fantastic sense of humour.'

Alexander Lubbock did the Lovaas programme when he was tiny, and his father feels that it gave him a fantastic kick-start. 'It is tremendously intense; we had five therapists and 40 hours a week of one-to-one for him. Each therapist does exactly the same thing with exactly the same words until the child gets it right five times out of five with each therapist, whatever the task is, and then they move on to the next thing. It just cuts through the glass ceiling.'

Alexander went on to attend school, which is the aim of most parents who do the home programme. There are a few opportunities to pursue ABA in schools that have been set up by parents, so that, at the age of five, children can go there and continue what they have learned at home. It is a flexible programme that can last for as long as it is needed.

To find out more about the programme, and get information about the possibility of funding options, contact Child Autism UK (01344 882248; www.childautism.org.uk), a parent-led charity which promotes early behavioural intervention for young children with autism using ABA.

The EarlyBird Programme

The EarlyBird programme run by the National Autistic Society lasts three months and consists of group training sessions for parents, combined with individual home visits where video feedback helps parents apply what they learn while working with their child. It supports parents at what can be a difficult time – after diagnosis and before school placement – and helps them to understand and deal with their child's autism in a way that will help his behaviour and social communication as well as giving invaluable contact with others in the same boat. 'The support of going for ten weeks and having a speech and language therapist, educational psychologist and someone within our borough who knew where to access help and support groups and so on was invaluable,' says Lesley Burton, who found the support on offer a great feature of the course, which she took at a vulnerable time just after her son's diagnosis of autism.

EarlyBird Centre (01226 779218) – details on www.autism.org.uk.

Home-Start

This is a brilliant scheme where a helper will befriend you and give you support. A volunteer from the organisation, who is a parent who has been specially trained for the work, comes to your house and helps you to cope with your child so you don't feel so alone. I had one – she would come around, make me a coffee, make sure I got a break while she would play with all the children, not just Matt. It was just what I needed. Find out more through your social worker or at www.home-start.org.uk.

Portage

This is a pre-school home visiting service in which a Portage worker will regularly visit you to show you how to do interactive play and learning activities with your special needs child and advise on some aspects of childcare. Then you practise the activities, which are all based on play, between visits, and report on your child's progress. You can get information on the service through your health visitor or from the National Portage Association (www.portage.org.uk). Portage teachers generally have great experience with ASD children and can give you masses of useful advice and support. I think you and your child will both benefit if you start on this as early as possible, before the child gets set in ways and habits. One of the best things about it is the emphasis on what parents can do for their children with appropriate encouragement.

Hanen

Hanen programmes (run by specially trained Speech and Language Therapists) are based on a Canadian system that aims to teach parents and other caregivers ways to promote children's language development during everyday activities. Find out more at www.hanen.org.

Makaton

Makaton is a language programme in which the most frequently used words are matched to sign language signs and clear picture symbols, all combined to promote communication and encourage language development in children with communication difficulties. At first signs are used and then gradually, if things go according to plan, the signs are dropped and speech takes over. Training programmes in this straightforward system are available for subscribing parents (ask your social worker about help towards the course) and follow-up support is available from a network of trained professionals. Details on www.makaton.org (01276 606760). I did one of the courses, and found it a great help, especially for parents whose child doesn't have much communication. Don't be nervous about doing this course. Sitting in a classroom singing a nursery rhyme and signing it at the same time is really great. All the children seem to join in, even those who are severely autistic – this is inclusion in action.

Early diagnosis makes a difference

With three children on the autistic spectrum, diagnosed at different ages and stages, Clare Ryan is well able to attest to the value of early intervention. Her oldest daughter, now 19, was only diagnosed in Year 6 at school when she was aged ten. It was a bit late by then and was not picked up until things were going quite badly wrong.

'Concern had started in nursery where they thought she was very well behaved but she didn't play, she just wanted to work. She was always very anxious. She is very bright but working out the social world exhausts her. Children like her can work things out cognitively but not emotionally. Most kids pick things up by osmosis; my children have learned to ask "Do you really mean that?" So many things are baffling to them.

'My youngest child was diagnosed much earlier, which made a huge difference. He is a much happier child because he was understood early. When he was 15 months old he regressed and stopped talking. I knew he was autistic. At two and a half I took him to a speech and language therapist and got his communication assessed. I then took the report to a paediatrician and by age three he was diagnosed.

'Early intervention strategies have really helped him, and that is clear when I compare with how his sisters, who were diagnosed at different, much later, stages have fared. It helped that his siblings understood autism and didn't bat an eyelid when he needed to flap, jump or watch TV standing on his head.'

3

All about Matt

In the first edition of this book, this chapter, all about Matt and his funny ways, was designed to help parents spot similar things about their own children, and see if our ideas might help them.

We were working on the basis that children with ASD all have their own distinct personalities, yet at the same time there are many characteristics that they seem to have in common. Because of this, we are going to retain a lot of the information about young Matt, and chart his progress with descriptions of how he is now. Wherever you are with your child you may find some things that you recognise – and some hope for the future.

Family life has certainly changed a lot on our journey with Matt. He was 14 when we first wrote this book and now he is 24, 6ft 1 and he is keen on tattoos. He has one that says 'Your thoughts and your feelings create your life', which comes from a book he read, and he really loves it.

He is funny and loves to be with lots of people. He has made so many friends when travelling and working. Everybody gets on with him, as he is so kind, gentle, caring and funny. I just cannot explain him any better than by saying he is becoming a wonderful man, and I am proud of all that he has achieved.

Matt then

> ## How it feels to be autistic by Matthew Keith Brealy, 14
> *'I don't know how you feel so how can I say how I feel? I feel normal thank you.'*

Looking back at teenage Matt, I see a boy who liked music, cars and enjoying life to the max. Matt did not like school very much and, like most teenagers, couldn't wait to leave. Matt liked things his way and to know exactly when/where/how things were going to happen. He forgot to finish things you gave him to do, like chores around the house or washing himself using soap.

Matt's temper was hot and cold. One minute he was happy, the next he was destroying his room; anything could trigger him off.

Matt liked to socialise with his mates as much as possible, which was very nice to see. He was a very caring boy to his family and would do anything to help when he knew you really needed him. Matt would say exactly what was on his mind to anyone. If you asked him 'Do you like my dress?' you had to be sure you really wanted the answer that he would give you!

> ## At home by Matthew Keith Brealy, 14
> *'Well I have one sister and two brothers so my Mum finds it hard so would I if I was in her position. I have my own room because I used to keep my older brothers awake so now I have been put in my new room sometimes my Mum and Dad find it hard to look after me because they have to keep repeating things what I do not understand and maybe when I have fits it must be scary to watch it happen. Well we all manage and they help me a lot and so do my older brothers and my little sister.'*

ASD children's senses are not the same as ours. When Matt was little, every day was a new day for all the impressions that he got, and each everyday thing that he saw was a new thing. He was always smelling and tasting things in the house and garden or at the shops, as a way of getting to know them. As a teenager, he would say something like 'You've changed the colour of the washing-up liquid' rather than having to taste it. That was after many years of telling him not to do it. His sense of taste is quite different – he found some sweet things bitter and he can't stand to eat anything slimy.

Matt smelled things very quickly – people or things. A lot of his judgements on people were based on smell, touch or other senses. His way of identifying things had to be very physical. He had to know what everything he encountered smelled and tasted like. Even clothes. If you came into the house he would know if you smelled different to normal. For instance, if something had been at my sister's house and then it came back with me, Matt would know that it had been there. So some of his senses were very, very sharp compared to what might be considered the norm.

Really, all his senses are a bit different. His hearing was so sensitive when he was small that he couldn't stand the noise of fireworks, or anything like that. He could never bear the touch of a hat. When he was a baby he would bite, scream and scratch when I put his hat on, and, of course, with no idea of the problem, I would keep putting it back on. When older, he would put a hat on himself but he still hated anybody touching his head. Matt's sight and visual perception were affected. The way he looked at things was different. He sometimes felt as if he saw ceilings or walls closing in on him.

Matt's pain threshold is different from ours, so he would do things like hurt his sister to see why she cried. When he was small, he put his hand on the heater and held on to it until he had burned his hand so badly it was totally blistered. He didn't have the wiring to make him feel pain like we do so he was puzzled and asked things like 'Why do you cry when you hit your head?'

Pain by Matthew Keith Brealy, 14

'The one good thing about having autism is I don't feel pain like you. I had my finger shut in a door and had to have lots of needles put in my fingernail but it did not hurt. I also had a nail go through my finger everyone was worrying about it but I got it out with Dad's pliers. It was ok, that made me laugh because everyone else had worried faces.'

Matt has always liked music. With music you play the notes and it comes out how you are playing them. He likes the structure. He was never allowed to learn piano at primary school because he was so far behind academically, but when he did start piano lessons it was clear that he had a natural talent.

He picked up the guitar by himself, and he even learned to play the drums. He loved listening to music and he could analyse it and tell me all about the structure, which at first amazed me because we were not really a musical family.

How the others saw 14-year-old Matt

Ben (21): *'At the end of the day he is my brother. I would look after him and make sure he is ok. He is harder to control than a normal brother – you have to tell him about 70 times not 20 to do something. When he was younger it was hard as he was in the same bedroom, and all night he was shouting or doing something, and this was hard to cope with.'*

Paul (18): *'He was hard to deal with when he was small. I felt Mum was with him more than me, but I know now that she had to be with him. It was a nightmare when we shared a bedroom. Now I find he tries to copy me – he mimics me when out or at home. I love him to bits but sometimes I have to stop and look at him and count to ten, as I know it is not his fault that he is a pain or doing something wrong. I will always be there for him no matter what he does – he's my bro.'*

Zoe (10): *'I find it hard to do things with him as he gets frustrated. He scares me by jumping out of the cupboard, which I hate. I will tell him what to do when he gets older to help him, as he needs it. When he has fits I get scared but I have to get used to it and learn what to do when this happens. When I was younger and needed Mum's help and Matt needed her too, I used to say "help Matt first".'*

Keith (Matt's dad): *'At first I blamed myself for Matt's problems, sometimes seeing myself in the things that he does, but over time, and with Jackie's determination, we have realised that Matt will not succeed in life skills unless we help him. I now look back over the years with a smile because of all the things that Matt has done: kept me awake at night with his night terrors, insisting that I put him to bed and make sure there are no spiders in the room and that his curtains are right, teasing me constantly and keeping me on my toes, as he often says. Matt has become a loving, caring teenager and I am proud of his determination to do things. Being a teenager is a difficult time for any child and Matt is having some problems dealing with this time in his life but he knows that he can turn to me if he needs help or fatherly advice. I love him to bits, after all he is my son!'*

My family by Matthew Keith Brealy, 14

'I love Ben as a brother I will help him if he needs me, I like it when he helps me out when I am in trouble, I can phone him and he will come and help me.

'I understand Paul more than anyone he knows a lot more than other people, he has been there and done it. I love him a lot. Paul will always help me out, even if he has important things to do, he always puts family first. Paul has taught me to stick up for myself, if I got beaten up he would come and sort it out.

'Zoe has helped me out with lots of things like reading, homework and I will always look after her. She makes me laugh when I am upset and I love her.

'Mum is very helpful and has kept me in school throughout the years she has taught me a lot of things to do and what not to do. She tries her best to treat me like any other kid (like my brothers) what I am glad of. Mum lets me do things so I have had a go at anything, even things that scare me.

'Dad helps me out a lot he treats me like a son but talks to me like a best mate, he has taught me to be careful and he lets me do most things that anyone else can do. He has made me more aware of things and has given me a taste of the real world. We have a good laugh together.'

Matt now

So how has Matt changed over the last ten years? For a start he has finished college and is a qualified bricklayer. He took some time out of work and went travelling with his friends. They travelled through Thailand and Vietnam on bikes and loved it. A few things Matt had to do worried him but he conquered every single thing. I am so very proud of him, as he never gives up and always finds a way to do everything he wants to do.

He lives independently now, renting a place with his girlfriend. He pays his rent and I help with food sometimes, but he is getting so much better with that. He has made some of his own furniture out of pallets and it looks great.

As always with ASD youngsters, you have to show them first, and explain things to them, and then let them do things for themselves. There are a lot of aspects of independent living that people with ASD find particularly hard. Matt worries if he has not paid a bill, and he will get very stressed over this and very cross. It usually happens if he has over-spent and has not budgeted for something. But he comes to us and we help him sort it out, then if it happens again he will know what to do.

In the family his oldest brother, Ben, has emigrated to Australia with his partner and our two grandsons. Matthew dealt with this very well as Ben had already moved out of the house, so his going away did not affect Matt's routine. I think this helped him to get used to the idea of us all not being in the same house, which is more difficult for someone like Matt than it would be for a non-ASD person.

Tragically, Paul, the brother closest to Matt in age, was killed in a car crash. We will talk about this in Chapter 8 under the heading of Bereavement. Matt's younger sister, Zoe, is studying to be a dental nurse.

Zoe (20): *'Matty has turned into a caring and loving brother who shows affection and support when needed and always brings a cheerful attitude with him. As he has grown up he has learned to deal with day-to-day life on his terms.'*

4

How ASD affects the family and relationships

Getting a diagnosis for your child is only the beginning. This is something that will have repercussions throughout the family, and how your extended family responds may have an impact on how you feel about them. No two families are alike, but from my own experience, and the things I have been asked in my work with other families, I find that some questions crop up over and over again. So I'll tell you about the things that happened to us, what I think we got right, and even some of the things that went a bit wrong.

I have learned a lot from the experience of bringing up Matt, both from the point of view of a parent trying to find the best way through the maze and because the challenges have led me back into education myself. I have done a number of courses and have taught special needs children as a learning support assistant.

When Matt was born my older sons, Ben and Paul, were six and three respectively and I had been with my husband, Keith, for 18 months. We had settled happily into being a family unit. I used to love those days when we would pack up a picnic or go to the beach just without thinking about it. If we had people round it didn't matter. In retrospect, life was really easy in those days. The boys were so excited about having a new brother, and when Matt was born they adored him. We sometimes feel that we have been tested to the max as a family since then.

When is the best time to tell your child they are autistic?

I don't think Matt knew he was different when he was small. It was only as he was growing up that he would ask questions like 'Why am I different?'

I didn't want Matt to have excuses in his mind for not doing things, so I told him about aspects of his condition as he needed to know them. It is too easy for these children to blame the ASD for everything. It becomes a way of not dealing with things. On the other hand, when they are older it can be quite a relief to understand their condition better and to discover 'oh, that's why I do this'.

- Observe your child and see if the understanding is there before you talk to him about it; ask him if he knows what autism is.
- Try to give him a positive image of himself. Use family photos and videos in which your child features, and talk about events he has taken part in so that he can see the role he plays in activities.

How do you explain to a child what autism is?

I did it in stages with Matt. I started by explaining, 'You think differently to other people, so you have to be a bit more patient with them and they have to be a bit more patient with you.' Then, when he was getting into arguments with people because he didn't understand what they were saying, I told him, 'They don't understand why you feel this way because you think differently to them.'

- Give a basic medical explanation of the condition, but keep it simple. Some books can help, but see what you think for your individual child, keep the explanation child-friendly, and don't go into the limitations ASD can impose.

What did Matt make of it?

The Christmas Matt was nine he wrote a letter to Santa. He gave me the letter and asked me if when I saw Santa I could ask him to keep his stocking and let him be normal for one day so he could see and feel like us. I kept the letter because it was so heartbreaking to realise how much he wanted to understand people and how different from everyone else he felt.

Hi Santa

I would Like to see you Some of my Friends say that your not true. I bleve in you are you my best Friend. I think that your the Kindess person ever. I have a promlam its horble its Like everone diffent than me. I would Like to Be you.

good bye

Frm matt

can I ask Some quaion quaion

1. want is it like going arael the woel.

2. How old ar you.

and I tried to be good you are a very nice man

That letter displays a kind of sensitivity that you wouldn't necessarily associate with the condition. I had to explain that Santa couldn't answer individual wishes like that, but I said I would try to help Matt understand. After that, when anything cropped up I would say, 'If that happened it would make me really happy, or really upset, or it would hurt me,' so that he could get some idea of the consequences of actions, and it showed him the difference between how he felt and how I felt in a particular situation.

- Help your child to understand other people's emotions. Collect up pictures from magazines and newspapers of people showing emotions such as anger, excitement and surprise, and talk about them.

Does an older child need to know more?

After Matt wrote his letter to Santa, I felt I needed to explain more about his condition. By the time he went to secondary school, he knew it had a name. I explained what it meant and some of the technical aspects of the condition. I told him about some of the famous people who were autistic, and other things that would help him to have a more positive impression. Then, luckily, there was something on television about a mathematical genius who had Asperger's. He watched it and accepted it all.

I didn't tell him the things that he would not be able to do. I told him that there was probably no point in his reading about it, as each person with autism is different, and while he might have some of the things they wrote about, equally, he might not have any of them. If he had wanted to know more, I would have highlighted the aspects that might apply to him and not have shown him any more than that. In fact, he didn't want to see anything. He knew that he would be able to do things like preparing his meals and having a job – we always emphasised the positive. As he got older, Matt became more analytical of the differences between him and us.

What to tell ASD children – and when

- Emphasise the positive in terms of what they *can* do.
- Tell them about famous people who have had the same condition: there is speculation that such well-known figures from the past as Albert Einstein, Isaac Newton and even Andy Warhol may have displayed behavioural patterns linked to ASD.
- Each child is different, but for almost all of them it will be a relief to know that there is a reason why they feel the way they do.
- You don't have to tell them everything at once. You will know best how much they can take in at any given time, and how much it is helpful for them to know about the condition.
- It may help to explain how you feel in particular situations and how it is different to how they feel.

The best time to tell your child they have ASD by Matt Brealy, 24

'I was glad when Mum and Dad told me I was on the autistic spectrum. I felt that it helped me understand a lot more, about the condition in general and myself in particular. If you had to tell someone else about your Asperger's syndrome you should just tell them if they ask, sometimes it will just come up in conversation. To be honest I've never had an issue telling someone.

'ASD children will probably gather that something is different about them by the time they are nine or ten. You are going to the doctor and stuff and mostly you will put two and two together by that age. But people are all different. I knew about it at 14, but others might be older. There is probably no ideal age to have the conversation – you need to go by each individual.'

Explaining ASD to your child

As the mother of an academically gifted Asperger sufferer, Finni Golden felt the same as I did when it came to telling her son, Jamie, about his condition:

'Knowing that Jamie has Asperger's has made a huge difference to both of us; the worry that he had when he couldn't understand why he was different and why he found things so difficult was far worse. Once you know that you have a problem you can address it and it is part of knowing who you are. He suffers badly with obsessive compulsive disorder as well, but I never made him think that he was ill; I just explained that everyone has tidiness parameters and all these other things but there are always going to be people who are off the scale and that he is a little bit off the scale, and then I told him about some scientific research, which helps to explain how he is about things. They did an experiment where they showed people with Asperger syndrome flash cards of an object and then a face. In a "normal" brain you analyse the face and expressions in a different area of your brain to a table or chair, whereas with someone with Asperger's it all goes into the same place. This may be why they can't read facial expressions and also why they are not considerate of other people's feelings. My son is enormously good company and he is very funny so there is absolute delight alongside all the horrendous things.'

A positive outlook

Kate, the mother of Jack, a teenager with Asperger syndrome, explains when they told him:

'It was clear from quite an early age that there was something different about Jack, and we suspected Asperger's. We always tried to focus on the positives when we talked to him about it – that there was something called Asperger syndrome that helped him to think and focus clearly and meant that he could really concentrate for long periods of time – and then, sometimes, we would say that I thought I had a touch of it myself. So that by the time Jack was actually diagnosed he already saw Asperger's as being a positive thing. We know that it brings with it loads of things – some fantastic, some quite tricky to deal with. When you are young you are so focused on the things that are causing you problems that you don't see the positives. But that huge ability to focus and to think clearly is an advantage that you can see as you get older.'

Siblings of ASD children

When do you tell siblings and how can you expect them to react?

My advice to parents would be to explain as soon as you can. Start by keeping it simple. Depending on their ages, you could just say something like 'Your brother is different and we can all help him in different ways.' As the siblings get older you can explain more. Younger siblings have to get used to it all bit by bit. You need to explain that lots of things that they do without thinking – like making eye contact, taking turns and understanding what other people are thinking and feeling – are very hard for their brother or sister with an ASD.

Mine knew quite early on – before Matt did, really – and our youngest child, Zoe, who is five years younger than Matt, knew there was something different about her brother from a very early age. She was quite a laid-back baby and if she heard Matt scream she would automatically be quiet. I could deal with him and then go back to her, even if I had been in the middle of feeding her, which is not normal, but was just what I needed. I thought she was sent from heaven. When she was about three, if Matt was in a state she would say 'Mummy go to Matt first' because she knew I had to sort him out, and she still has a lot of patience with him to this day.

The older two found it very hard sometimes when they were younger. Matt used to upset them with things like tearing up their homework and keeping them awake at night. Just try telling your teacher that your brother has destroyed your homework. It may be a novel twist on 'the dog ate it' but it does not go down any better. He would take something from one brother and put it in the other one's bag because he found it fascinating to see them getting angry. When they were all sharing a room he would swap their teddy bears around when they were asleep. It was all quite ingenious, but he really just wanted to see what would happen. He would let the tyres down on their bikes just to see if it would irritate them. Children are very territorial with their things – Matt would sit back and just find it funny. Of course, all that was hard for young boys to cope with, but as they got older they coped really well.

How do you keep the family balance when the siblings inevitably don't get enough attention?

We didn't go out as a family nearly so much when Matt's behaviour started to be challenging. We didn't go on camping holidays with the children until he was older as we knew he couldn't cope with it, which meant that the others missed out. They always had to wait. I think Matt's siblings missed out on normal family social life. It took me a long time to get back into any kind of normal pattern.

The important thing is, we are a family and we are all in it together. Our oldest son never resented it; the next one down needed more time than I had to give him and I think he did resent that. He was a very sensitive child and he needed me a lot more. He used to get cross with me and say 'You spend all your time with Matt.' I have always regretted it, and you can never put that time back. As he got older he knew that he could pick times when I would be there for him. He had to learn how to choose those times.

It was always, 'Can you do that for yourself? I've just got to go and see to Matt.' The boys used to say, 'It's Matt, Matt all the time.' I would suddenly ask, 'Where is he?' and he would be upstairs drinking the bleach. I could lock it away but he was so smart at finding keys, climbing things, anything. I thought it had to stop because the other children were not having the family life they should have been having. That was when the respite care came in, and it was so important to us that I am going to discuss it at length in Chapter 5.

How much can your other children be expected to contribute to the care of a sibling with problems?

Growing up with a brother with special needs has made my children more aware of people around them. It has given them more empathy towards other people. If your children have never been in contact with it, they don't know how to react to disability of any kind and I think that puts them at a disadvantage.

However, we were always thinking about where Matt was, what he was doing, how he was behaving, and that went on for a long time. Matt didn't think before things happened and he always was that way.

Siblings may find that, as in our family, the ASD child will connect most strongly with one of them. Matt's closest relationship was always with my second son, Paul, the nearest to him in age. Matt always had a real admiration for him. When Matt went to his brothers' school Paul was very protective of him, which Matt loved, and as Paul was quite a streetwise boy no one messed with him. If Matt was ever bullied, as soon as the perpetrators realised that Paul was his brother, they left Matt alone. Paul also helped him sort right from wrong. I would always ask Paul to chat with Matt if I felt I was not getting through to him.

Are sibling support groups helpful?

I found a group for the siblings of autistic or Asperger's children, and the older boys went together. All the children could freely ask the doctor what they wanted to know, so the boys found out some of the reasons why Matt did the things he did, which made them feel less alone. Afterwards, when they had talked to other children who were in the same boat as they were, they understood Matt much better, asked me lots of questions about his condition and treatment, and had more patience with him. It might be better for children who are shy of groups to talk to a child psychologist on an individual basis – at any rate, siblings do need some kind of help. You have to take their feelings into account.

How do you tell the extended family?

Once we knew the truth about what was the matter with Matt we had to think about how we would explain it to the family, which was one of the hardest battles. We had different types of reaction from them. Some of them were quite accepting; others seemed to take the view that any special needs children should be in homes, which was very upsetting. You do have to remember that an older generation may struggle to accept the idea of a condition that was not recognised in their time, especially when their grandchild looks perfectly normal. All the grandparents found it hard to accept at first. It took a long time for them to see that Matt is different, not just naughty, but they came to accept him for the person he is.

For a while we felt we couldn't take Matt anywhere within the family because of the way they reacted. A lot of the family found his condition baffling until they had learned more about it. Keith's dad always had a particularly good bond with Matt and always understood his anxieties and needs. He drove him to school and was very considerate, trying to stick to the familiar routes, and letting Matt beep the horn on the corners as he was convinced that this was what you were supposed to do, so he got cross if it wasn't done. My mum was good about understanding his communication problems, and would repeat sentences when he needed her to. All his grandparents found it easier once Matt got a bit older and they could clearly see the ways he was different from his peers and the problems he would face. His cousins will always look out for him, which is great as I will not always be here and I want him to be able to live normally but know he can get help if he needs it from people who care about him. His siblings know how he will need them later on in life. The special bond makes them a stronger family unit and I feel I have done well here.

Family lessons

- You need support from your family – be honest and try to make them understand what they can do to help you.
- Tell your other children sooner rather than later.
- Find a support group, if at all possible, and talk to others in the same position as you. In the first instance contact the National Autistic Society helpline (0808 800 4104).

- Investigate local sibling support groups (we were referred by our paediatrician) and try to find one for the right age range for your children.
- There will be behaviour that upsets siblings: be prepared to help them understand and deal with it.
- Timetable in time to be with your other children – they need you, too.
- If you feel that your child would like to have friends, be proactive in helping establish bonds with other children.
- Investigate the possibilities for respite care – it will help you to restore some balance in the family. Use the time to do family things and ask your other children what they would like to do.
- Go to talks on autism and learn about it.
- It is not the end of the world. Try to be happy with it yourself.

How does the situation affect your friendships?

I found it hard at diagnosis. Some friends accepted it and were supportive, some – not the ones I would have expected – cut me off. It hurt when I felt that I had lost some friends at such a personally vulnerable time. Some friends we have now are very fond of Matt and accepted the way he is, so we were relaxed when they were around, and Matt's godmother was a tower of strength.

What is awful to start with is that tense feeling with your child when you are out, wondering if he will behave, or what he will do next – like a toddler time-bomb but **all** the time. It does make you tense and defensive, but as you get more used to it you do find out what works and what doesn't as far as social life is concerned. It is best to compromise a bit and not put yourself under pressure to keep your old life as it was.

The boys went through a stage where they were embarrassed to bring friends home because of Matt, but as they got older they learned to deal with his behaviour and would tell mates before they arrived at the house, 'My brother is different, don't be offended if he says something odd – he's a great guy but he is not like us.'

How can friends help?

Most of our friends just accepted that this was the way we were as a family. I have a good friend who I can always chat to when I need a sympathetic ear and she would listen and we could have a joke about things. She would never judge me as a parent but would always help. What you need in this situation is support, not advice. Sometimes, when I felt a bit overwhelmed, she would drag me out for a girly evening, which did me a world of good. Some friends built up a rapport with Matt and would take him for the day, though with some people it was too much worry even if they offered.

- Real friends will not judge you or your family. You know who they are, but remember it can sometimes be difficult for even good friends to understand, as they do not go through this each day like us.
- As a good friend, don't get upset if the child says something hurtful like 'I don't like your dress' – understand that he or she really doesn't mean to be rude.
- Be patient with the child.
- Be a good listener.
- Understand that all days are not the same.
- Don't judge the rest of the family because of this child.
- Volunteer to go with your friend who has an ASD child to meetings with health professionals and teachers, write down what they are saying and talk it through afterwards. Sometimes it is just too much for one person to take in on their own, and moral support is wonderful.

Your child's friendships

Can you help an ASD child to be more sociable?

The level of contact Matt has is not typical of Asperger sufferers, but right from the start I have helped him to socialise. When they said at nursery that he wasn't socialising, I felt that he had to have friends and we would have to help him get them. Having older brothers was the key because they would bring friends round and that meant that Matt could see the relationships and thought he would like the same for himself. So, when he started school, I invited children to tea so they could see him at home and it progressed from there. At first he couldn't face talking to other children, but he learned how to through his brothers.

- Have family meals and be strict about making your ASD child do their best to join in – they are part of the family, and this is a first step towards an outside social life.
- When they find it hard, get the others to go at the ASD child's pace and let them talk without interruption.
- Help them to want to interact with other people by teaching them some useful social skills, such as how to join in a conversation, where to stand and so on.
- Encourage them to play with other children – board games (perhaps with a sympathetic adult at first while they get the idea) and outdoor games and activities such as trampolining.
- Join Cubs, swimming clubs, drama or music groups – it all helps.

What about unsuitable friendships?

Matt is very different from some Asperger's people in that he is sociable and he loves his friends, but unfortunately the children he mixed with were very outgoing and game for a laugh, and sometimes they exploited his condition. They would suggest something and he would go off and do it, which could land him in trouble. I did worry about what they got up to but, on the other hand, I am glad he had friends. You can try to channel your child into a different direction with friendships, but ultimately, if you want them to have friends there is only so much you can do. You can try to socialise as much as possible with your child to push them in the direction of more suitable friendships, or find other children with the same interests. But you might come across some parents who will not let their child play with yours.

What can you do when a parent loses his or her temper with the child?

As a family we help each other. If someone dealing with Matt was starting to lose it we would hand over to someone else. You could do more harm than good if you tried to stick it out with him as you could easily raise his anxiety and that would lead to bigger problems.

- If you feel you are losing it, call time out for yourself. If you are on your own then say you will be back in ten minutes, and go to the bathroom just to cool off. When you return you will be able to see the problem more clearly as you will have had time to think.
- So that the child doesn't think they have won, you say to them with your hand up, 'Not discussing.' It is important for both of you that you are still in charge of the situation.

How can people outside the family cope with your child?

- Be patient!
- If you are left to look after the child it is most likely that you know them fairly well already, so plan ahead a bit and think of things you know they like to do.
- Know how to use the PECS picture symbols, if that is how they communicate, and make sure you know what the house rules and regulations are – this is important with any child, vital with ASD children.
- Remember to talk straight to the child, saying their name clearly first.

How to encourage children with ASD by Matt Brealy, 24

'If you get to know an autistic child well enough to find what their interests are, then encourage those interests instead of trying to force other things down their neck that they are not interested in, because if they are not interested they are not going to do it. Because they are straightforward in their thinking it is pretty much that simple.'

For some parents it is enough that they know what is causing their child's problems. They often don't seek formal diagnosis and don't voice their thoughts to their child, with the rationale that if the child thinks of himself as in some way disabled he will make less progress.

Being different

Jenny's nine-year-old son, Dan, has always been a quirky boy, but it is only in the last few years that his school has suggested that he might be on the autistic spectrum.

'When Dan was small I used to notice little things he did, like intently lining up his toys in a particular way, or walking on tiptoes, but I didn't think it was anything to worry about. It was only when he was six or seven that his teacher thought that he was doing and saying things that gave cause for concern. Dan sees things very much in black and white, and he was getting quite frustrated and obsessed with one subject to the exclusion of all else. To me it wasn't a problem but I was worried about him and whether other children wouldn't understand him.

'I felt that the way he was talking, getting frustrated and crying a lot were worrying, but when I contacted my family doctor they said that no pill would sort this kind of thing out, and if the teachers were saying he was on the spectrum then they should sort it out. There was no offer of any help so up to now I have left it at that, though I have some real worries about Dan's transition to secondary school, and whether that will be hard for him. I do think it will be best for him to stay in the mainstream.

'I have never discussed Dan's condition with him. He knows he is a bit quirky, but I haven't told him why. He has lots of friends, but he is happy in his own company out of school. He is a very good singer but won't join the choir. He is happy in his own little world. His friends do notice things about him. He knows all about films and film directors, and they always turn to him if they have any questions on the subject. So I can see benefits as well as disadvantages in the way he is. I have never felt that it is a problem that I have to deal with.

'I have noticed that he is rocking more than he did. He says that he knows he needs to keep that kind of thing under control when he is at school, but has to let it out when he gets home. He is a happy child, so at the moment I am keeping things as they are. It is a question of finding someone who can help him.'

I would always respect a parent's feelings about what is right for their child, and we are not all the same, as is only too clear from everything in this book. However, in this case, I think there might be a lot to be said for action. Dan sounds like a very bright little boy, and he knows himself that he is different, so if he understood why, it might be a relief for him. For instance, if he understood why he was rocking then he might be able to change it to tapping or something else that suits him but is less extreme. I think he probably rocks at home more now for comfort because his anxiety levels are rising at school as he gets older and things get more complicated.

He is bright enough to know that he has to keep it to a home activity but when he gets to big school, I can see his anxiety increasing as there are so many more children there to deal with. I would recommend that they have an assessment done as soon as possible so that they know for sure what they are working with and then I think Jenny should be trying to get things organised to ensure a smooth transition to his next school. It doesn't sound as if they have had much joy from the health service, so it might be worth trying to access help from an educational psychologist through the school in the first instance.

5

Coping emotionally and getting support

Bringing up a child with an autistic spectrum disorder has many rewards but, make no mistake, it can be a relentlessly draining process. You need a lot of support from family and friends, and even then, a short break from time to time may be the best thing for you and your family. For this reason, I am going to write at length about respite care at this point, because it made all the difference to my family.

Respite care can be a lifeline

When Matt was eight, the social services said we could have respite care and when I asked the children what they thought about it they said, 'Does that mean we could have a normal weekend just with you?' That clinched it, really. Respite brought the closeness back – I hadn't realised quite how much our family life had been compromised.

Respite care involved Matt going to someone else for one long weekend a month. It made a huge difference to our family, and was a crucial step in restoring some balance to our family life, and giving the other children the attention they needed. It meant that I could do things with them to make up for all the time when I was concentrating on Matt. I felt I needed to have some time with the other children just to have an uninterrupted chat. We would go out for walks and just do things on the spur of the moment, which was normally impossible, and if we wanted to play a game, we could without Matt disrupting it. Such simple things, but they meant a lot to us. We really needed that precious family time when we could just relax.

Matt used to accept the respite care fantastically. As he got older he didn't like it so much but we kept it going because the other children needed it. I think in a way it helped him to mature because it was good for him to have to make the effort with someone outside the family and to accept that things are different at another house. He always went to the same person. It is definitely worth trying to set up an arrangement like this if you can, and you should be able to do so through the social services.

Initially, I felt very inadequate to be asking for help, as if it meant that I couldn't cope as a mother, but unless you live with a child like Matt you can't really appreciate the stresses of the situation. It is hard as a parent to say, 'I can't cope.' I made myself say it in the mirror and somehow saying it to myself like that made a difference. I think that in some ways it is a sign of strength to be able to acknowledge that you need some help, and it is better for the whole family if you decide to get what you can. When I first spoke to a social worker she asked if I wanted Matt put into foster care. Of course, nothing was further from my mind: all I was asking for was respite, which is not the same at all. My advice to anyone who thinks that respite care might be the answer is to speak to your key worker about it and keep trying. Don't be put off if you have a long wait. You need to establish a continuity of care and make sure that any discipline you have established is reinforced. Bear in mind that older children may have different needs and might want to move on from one-to-one care to something more socially inclined and outward-looking.

Parents fall into a trap if they feel that they are the only ones who can possibly have a special relationship with their child; it can be so beneficial to have another adult who is involved. I can understand how parents get so stressed if they are coping alone. Help should be forthcoming straight away if parents need it, though of course it often isn't. You shouldn't be put on a waiting list when you are desperate.

People with ASD are all different. It is important to remember that, apart from all having idiosyncrasies, they have their own personalities. Different things trigger them and you can't have too many preconceived rules when you are caring for them. You can expect too much from those with ASD who are good at communicating, and, as they do not look disabled, people can have unrealistic expectations. Make sure that your respite carer understands this.

Different types of respite care

Various kinds of care are available to help you, most of which require local authority funding, and not all of which are available to everyone. You can find out more from your local social services, or the NAS website is a good place to start looking.

- Home-based respite care.
- Family-based short-term respite, which is similar to foster care. A disabled child is matched with a family and then stays with them on a regular basis.
- Children's homes which offer residential short-term care which gives respite to families.
- After-school activities, youth clubs, play schemes and summer camps.
- Residential schools.
- Befriending schemes run by the National Autistic Society through its volunteering network (01159 113369 for details).

When respite care is needed

Lesley, mother of autistic teenager Eddie, feels that he has got to an age and stage where respite care might be beneficial.

'We are looking into occasional respite now that Eddie is older, as, if he got used to it, it would really do him good. Also, it will be good for the rest of the family to have a chance to recharge our batteries and have a bit of a life outside of Eddie.

'His school takes Eddie camping. It is something they do every year. For six weeks beforehand they take them to the site and show them where to eat and sleep, etc. They do all kinds of walking, climbing, obstacle courses, and sleep in a tent. He was wobbly at first but he did it and had a real sense of achievement, and it was really good for him. Camping is great, as it is a means by which Eddie is getting used to being away from home. I think that this will really help him to slot into respite.'

Dealing with everyday stress

When I had a really bad day and snapped at Matt, my husband took over when he got home so I could shut off for a while. I would try to make sure I had an hour a day to relax, away from all the constant questions and so on. I think it is very important to get a break; the relentlessness of the condition can be exhausting for carers and that is why it can be so much harder for single parents if they don't have anyone else who can take over for a while.

Timetable some stress-relief

One thing that can help you long term is to make a note of which parts of the day are most stressful for you, perhaps by making a chart that you fill in every day for a while. If all the family members do this, you will fairly quickly be able to see which parts of the day are the low points, and try to organise extra help, perhaps from extended family and friends, at these times. Perhaps Grandpa can give the children a lift to an evening activity, or a friend can sit with your ASD child for an hour while you go to yoga – anything that stops you from feeling you are being split in two by the additional demands of the situation.

- Make sure you get a chance to relax when the children have all gone to bed – a long soak in the bath, a glass of wine, an outing with a friend – you deserve a reward and this is your time.
- This can be harder for single parents, but do what you can – phone someone for a chat, or get a friend to come round to you.
- Sign up for a Home-Start helper to give you a morale boost.

Safeguarding relationships and coping as parents

Your relationship with your partner is very special and you need to make sure you have time for yourselves. Looking after your family, and in particular your ASD child, is a very demanding job, and you need a break from time to time, in this job more than most. Here are a few tips to think about.

- Go out for a meal together or have a special meal at home with no interruptions.
- Find a babysitter you can trust so you can relax when you are out.

- Go on a picnic or for a walk together when the children are at school.
- If you are lucky with family who will look after the kids then have a few days away – just the two of you.

You both need time together. If you don't make time you will risk the rows happening and this is no good for you or your family. If you are a single parent, you need some relaxation time even more. Don't ever be too proud to ask family and friends for help, and for their time.

The mixed emotions you have as a parent of a child with special needs are awful; guilt haunts you. There are lots of trigger points. I felt very low at first when we had the diagnosis, but I knew I had to square up to it, and I did. Keith found it incredibly hard. Matt was his first child. He was devastated and blamed himself and it took him a long time to come to terms with it. I was the one who went to all the meetings and the talks and told him what I had learned. Usually it was the mums at the meetings. Most men find that sort of thing really hard, but Keith did think it was comforting that there were other dads like him.

Parents go through a stage of blaming themselves. In the end you just have to accept that this thing has happened. You get situations where the mother can't cope and the child goes into care or the father just walks away. The feelings of isolation are hard to bear. Support is crucial at this time. Be aware that it is not unusual to have irrational feelings of shame.

Sometimes you almost feel you are being victimised because you have had this child. That is so wrong: it is hard enough to accept that your child is different without having to fight for everything you need. Every person with children like this misses support and understanding from family when it is not there, but all the difficulties made Keith and me feel that our relationship was stronger than it was before. I could see where the pitfalls could break a relationship, and in fact a high percentage of marriages where a child in the family has special needs do break up.

Any condition that affects the mind is still a big taboo in parts of our society. I have been at the school gates waiting to pick Matt up when another parent has come up to me and said 'I don't wish my child to catch what yours has, so I don't want him anywhere near.' I did not bother to reply to this breathtaking ignorance but it still left me embarrassed and upset. On another day we were having lunch when we were shopping and Matt had an epileptic fit. A woman came up to us and said, 'It puts me off my food; you should not bring a child like that out.' It just made me despair.

As a parent you have to accept that your child is different, and this can take time. Once you have grieved over the loss of a normal, healthy child you can start again. Parents do need some time to come to terms with everything. Don't rush it, you need to understand the situation you are in yourself, then you can see what you can do to help. I soon found my feet when putting my energy into helping Matt. Now I am so proud of my family but most of all I am proud of Matt, as he has come so far.

- Give yourselves time to come to terms with the situation – this is a hard time and you need to square up to it.
- Don't be too proud to ask for help and support.
- Contact a Family is a nationwide charity giving advice, information and support to parents of disabled children, and helping parents to contact other families locally and nationally. Helpline: 0808 808 3555, www. cafamily.org.uk.

6

Communication

A Lego™ game will make you think

If we always remember the need to explain things to our ASD children, it might make life much easier. There is an exercise we did in my training for an NVQ in special needs that I think everyone should try. Two people each have the same little Lego™ set to assemble, but they cannot see each other. One has to assemble the set using only the instructions they are given verbally by the other. I would be amazed if anyone gets this right first time. It just shows how difficult it can be to communicate everything to another person. You have to explain all the things you normally do automatically; you have to explain each and every step of the way. Once you have tried it you will realise how much we constantly assume that other people know, and you just can't do that with a child with ASD.

If you try this game yourself, be exact in your definitions, and keep remembering to say the other person's name, so they know you are talking to them. This leads me on to some key things to remember:

The golden rules of communicating with your ASD child

- Use the child's name repeatedly – they need to know that you are talking to them.
- Get the child's full attention and try to exclude background noise like the television so they can concentrate on you.

- Use simple language with no unnecessary words and say exactly what you mean – no fancy turns of phrase such as 'I'm hopping mad' or 'I laughed my head off' – remember these children are very literal-minded.
- Allow them the time they need to understand what you have said and process information.
- Give the child a reason to communicate, so that they can get something they want, whether it is food or a toy that you have put out of reach. From a very early age I got Matt to say what he wanted, not just point to it, so before he could have what he wanted he had to make an effort.
- Be definite in what you say, especially when it is about the time you will do things: 'We will go out straight after breakfast,' or 'You can watch television at five o'clock.'
- Use picture symbols or photos to communicate if that is easier for them (see Chapter 2).
- Be positive and tell them what they **should** be doing rather than what they shouldn't.
- Only promise things you can deliver.

I have learned quite a lot through doing specialised courses, and if parents have the time I recommend that they do the same. You can get details of courses from your local library or Further Education college or from the NAS website: www.autism.org.uk.

I used to work as a veterinary assistant and what sticks in my mind with my approach to Matt is how you train a dog. Those simple, straightforward instructions: 'Sit, now', 'Stay, now' were what we were limited to. With most children you assume they know certain things; with dogs you assume they know nothing, so that approach is not as daft as it sounds. It worked with Matt. 'Matt, hand, hold, now!' worked, where something more complex, abstract and confusing to him did not.

Tones of voice

Your child needs to understand that you will use different tones of voice for different situations.

- Normal voice when talking.
- Voice of authority, which is firm, for when they need control/discipline.
- Calming voice, lower than usual, to help them out of a tantrum or panic.

How to help your child develop conversation skills

- Give them lots of practice in how to start a conversation and then keep it going.
- Get them used to the idea of changing topics, and not holding forth at length on something that they find fascinating.
- Teach them not to talk for too long – perhaps you could practise with an egg timer.

Conversation can be a real problem with ASD children. Even when they are willing, they don't understand how to do it. These tips will help, especially with young teenagers.

- When you are in a group, have more than one of you talking in turns so they get used to and accept turn-taking in conversation.
- When you have friends round get them to do this while the youngster is watching.
- Once they have watched for long enough to get the idea, persuade them to join in by asking them a question.
- Make joining in attractive to them by focussing your conversation on something they love.
- Take them out into social areas and let them observe other children and what they are doing and how they are interacting. Find a club that is appropriate to some of their interests – say, trains, or birds, or sport, and take them somewhere that others are enjoying this activity. Make sure they are aware of what is going on and talk to them about how nice it can be to join in with other people who like the same things.
- Computers can give ASD children elements of a social life. They are not guessing what you mean by tone of voice and facial expression – the information is just there in words and images, and this levels out the playing field with other children. You do need to keep even more of an eye on what is happening to them on social networks than do most parents, and make them aware of what is safe and what is not. Make them a list of phrases, such as 'Would you like to meet up', from a stranger that they really should talk to you about first. See p118 for the issue of cyberbullying.

Socialising by Matt Brealy, 24

'I love socialising with people. I love the fact that we are all so different, and trust me I've met some strange people. I'm well into my music and love going to festivals so I'm constantly meeting new people. When you spend a lot of time with friends you can learn from them and watch them and that helps a lot as well. You know where your level is and you know that sometimes stuff you want to do or say just isn't appropriate. That is stuff you learn with age.'

Social struggles

Jack's mum, Kate, describes how he struggled with friendships:

'Jack found it hard to organise his own social life – in the end I stood back a bit from doing it all for him, but realised that he would almost prefer not to do anything than to have to organise things for himself. Finding it hard to read social signals makes this kind of thing very difficult for people with ASD, and on the phone Jack gets no clues from the person on the other end.

'When he was younger he struggled with friendships because his behaviour was so difficult, but now he is extremely popular. He no longer appears weird – he comes across as charmingly eccentric rather than a bit freaky (rather like Matt in that respect). Asperger's people are very loyal friends because they don't like anything to change. They can't do with all that complicated ever-changing playground politics, so they don't get involved in any of it. They don't understand it and they are never going to be able to play those games.

'Jack spent so long wanting to be empathetic and kind and thoughtful, and faking it because he just doesn't feel those things naturally, that now he has almost absorbed the behaviour and it has become a part of him. He is thoughtful and kind and a good listener because he has taught himself to be – and he is funny. He makes everybody laugh, he is bright, he knows stuff, he is interesting, and he has always got loads of friends, and makes friends really easily.'

Tips on how to help your teenager make social arrangements without too much pain

- Ask them to ring a friend to make an arrangement, and before the phone call write down what they need to say.
- Have the phone on loudspeaker so you can help them if necessary.
- Get them to think of things they would like to do – and friends who might like to join them.
- Go with them to their friend's house and help them to ask face to face – help them get used to the right formula of words to use.
- Encourage them to make arrangements themselves and guide them on how to do this by showing them how you arrange meeting up with your friends.

7

Behaviour

'That child needs a good slap!'

'That mother should be ashamed of herself letting him behave like that!'

Prepare to harden your heart; your child's behaviour is likely to bring out the intolerant worst in a lot of people. Of course, they don't know what they are talking about, or what you have to go through every day, and if they did I hope they would not be so quick to judge. Don't worry about what other people think. The important thing is that you deal with behaviour that you find a problem in a way that works for you and your child. I have found the best way to cope with things is by not moving boundaries. A child with ASD likes to walk a firm black line – that is what feels safe. If the child goes into a grey area, anxiety increases and you end up with a bigger problem. The important thing is that your rules have to stay the same at all times, no matter how hard this is to do. That way your child feels safe and you are in control.

Helping them to change bad habits

- Work out what you wish to change and why.
- Plan how you are going to do it.
- Explain to them why and how they need to change.
- Ask the family to help – if you are all consistent you can avoid giving crossed messages.
- Reward good habits – and when they have tried to stop doing something bad.

- Have goals they can reach.
- Make a reward chart together, so it can feature treats that relate to whatever they are into at the time.

Our aim was always to make sure that Matt really understood what we were trying to do. Sometimes going over things two or three times would be enough; sometimes we could be repeating something for months or years on end. If he dug his heels in straight away, we would always know we were in for a battle. In that case, the key was to see what was making him angry or confused.

- Assess your behaviour as well as theirs. Do you explain things in enough detail?

Flapping

Matt used to flap and shake his hands, as if he was frantically fanning his face with both hands. The need to flap is common among people with ASDs, along with similar repetitive self-stimulatory habits, known collectively as 'stimming'. Sometimes they do it through anxiety, sometimes through habit, sometimes for comfort. I usually found with Matt that he did it when he was anxious, and if he was left to it, it would lead into rocking, which always looked very disturbing.

If you have a child in a playground flapping his arms then other children will stare and be frightened, or puzzled, or amused, and in the same way, when you have a young man buying drinks at a bar and flapping his arms, they are quite likely to think he has had enough to drink already and refuse to serve him. None of these responses are what you want for your child when you are trying to integrate them into the world, so we wanted to modify the flapping to something a bit less conspicuous.

We developed a routine where I would just put my hand up, which was the stop signal, say 'Stop' gently but firmly in a low voice and then say 'Tap' and he would copy me and move his hands down to tap his leg instead, and then gradually we changed it to tapping his side. I wasn't taking his flapping away from him altogether but replacing it with another habit that was easier to cope with. He still taps on his side now, when he feels the need to, but it is not as obvious as somebody flapping their arms. He is still being allowed to flap or tap but it doesn't look so distinctive or odd to other people. It doesn't now have the look of something that people would see and judge him for. The tapping is much calmer and doesn't fuel his anxiety like the flapping did. Interestingly, when we got him out of the flapping habit, he stopped rocking, too. The whole thing has become much less extreme for him.

Flapping by Matthew Keith Brealy, 14

'I am glad my mum stopped me flapping because I would look like an abnormal kid and my mates would not like it.'

The reason that you might want to modify extreme habits is just so that your ASD child won't look so different in a society that is not very tolerant of difference. There is no reason that they should have to fit in with our society, but they will probably have a better time if they don't stand out from the crowd too much. This sort of modification will give them the best chance to fit in. It can take a very long time to establish. It took us 12 to 18 months to work on Matt's flapping to the point where it was hardly happening at all. You can't get someone with an ASD to stop doing things like that completely, because these habits are part of the way they meet the world, and also a relief for them.

For Matt the replacement activity gave the same degree of comfort, which is important. A lot of people tap on the side of their leg in time to music or whatever, so he did not stand out too much. For us, it was a slow, gentle modification. When you are trying to get your child to do something like this, which takes constant repetition of an instruction from you, you have to keep calm, and keep your voice very low and gentle, every time, and say something reassuring, like 'It's okay, you can bring your hands down, we can tap together.'

If other parents got cross or agitated when they were trying to deal with something like the flapping, then they would probably make it worse, and the child would do it all the more. All you are doing is giving the child even more anxiety, because they won't understand why you are saying 'stop'. These habits are important to ASD sufferers. They tend to like things like twiddling a pen, so, if you are teaching them, you give them a card for 'twiddle time' if they seem to need it. Give them five minutes off class work and then they know they are going back to work afterwards. So they still get things done, and if it is at a slower rate, what does it matter?

Tantrums

People with ASDs all have different habits, and there are some things you simply have to try to stop. If your child is having a tantrum on the floor, you go down to their level and in a very calm voice you hold out your hand and say 'Five, four, three, two, one, finished now, let's go and do something else.' So you have taken them away from what was making them panicky – for example, if they wanted to play with a ball or something else that wasn't there – just by changing the focus. You have stopped the tantrum calmly, and quietly given them something else to think about. Then say something like 'Ok, you can have five minutes with the ball and then we are going to do something else.' Then give them an egg timer and time it. When the time is up you do something else, just like you said you would. A lot of these techniques also work really well with children who are not on the autistic spectrum.

It helps your child, when they have got in a state, to have a familiar format. You are their safety net; if you get angry and move your boundaries around, they will get confused and they won't feel safe. If you keep the boundaries the same and say very firmly that you have asked them to finish their tantrum, then you have taken over where they have lost control, and they feel safe because you have told them what they are going to do and that it is something that they can manage. So you take their mind off what the tantrum was about – you tell them that you are going to paint now, or to play with a ball, and then you can deal with what caused the tantrum in the beginning. Maybe they were trying to do something that frustrated them because it was too difficult or beyond their age range.

Your strength is very reinforcing for your child, so you have to make sure that you can be strong. You have to stay calm with them all the time, even if inside you feel as if you are about to flip your lid. I have sometimes had to go into a different room and scream.

This type of behaviour often gets lumped under the heading of 'challenging behaviour' but I think that is entirely the wrong definition. ASD tantrums or panics are invariably a response to things that your child feels have gone out of control, an expression of unhappiness and fear. I would call challenging behaviour something that is proactive, and seeks a response – of course, you will probably have to deal with both types of behaviour from time to time.

ASD children do sometimes communicate emotions in a way that seems violent. They will generally only hit out as a response when something is bothering them. I do not think that this is challenging behaviour, just a basic reaction. A child with ASD could virtually strangle someone, not for any malicious reason but because they wanted to shut them up.

What to do if noise causes tantrums and anxiety

Matt would sometimes have tantrums when we were just sitting watching television, and it was hard to understand why. In the end I realised that he just couldn't bear loud noises and the tantrums always started when there was something like a police siren on television, and when that happened, he just wouldn't stay in the room. We tried to protect him from loud noises while we got him used to them so that they wouldn't cause him such problems.

We would always stay indoors on firework night because Matt really hated all the noise. Gradually, over a long time, we got as far as watching the fireworks on the doorstep and then, after even longer, we could watch them outside without Matt freaking out.

We helped Matt deal with the fear of noises by getting him to make loud noises himself, playing with pots and pans and, later, his brother's drum kit. Reacting to his problems and changing what **we** did rather than trying to change what **he** felt was always our best way of coping.

The art of dealing with noise

- Try playing music games.
- Take your child to music therapy to get them used to different types of noise.
- Go to the fire station and look at the fire engines – ask the firefighters to put on a siren if they are not too busy.
- Play at being police cars – crime fighting can get really noisy.

Incentives for good behaviour

- Choose incentives to help your child behave. If they are obsessed with a particular DVD for instance, let them watch it when they have behaved well.

- One incentive that worked well for us was this: Matt got £1 a night if he was where he should be at the right time, but he lost £1 if he was not. The same principle applied if we wanted him to behave better at school. He got £1 for a praise card from school, and lost £1 for a bad report.

The Golden Rules

An idea that is used a lot in school, and would work at home, too, is the 'golden rules'. These are behaviour points that are set out firmly in the class, and children are rewarded for their compliance. I made up my own set to use with Matt, which are aimed at autistic children, and you could make up your own to suit your child.

Matt is gentle.

Matt will listen to people.

Matt will put his toys away.

Matt does not hurt anyone.

Matt will not interrupt.

Matt will not leave his toys for someone else to tidy.

Matt will try hard at school.

Matt will not walk out of school.

Matt is kind to others.

Matt will not hurt the feelings of others.

What you can do when behaviour is a problem

- Use simple instructions – make sure they have really understood.
- Stay calm – especially when dealing with tantrums – if you get angry it will make ASD sufferers very anxious.
- If your child is clearly getting angry or upset, try to get them to go out to the garden or somewhere else that is safe – and make it easy for them to get there without too much in their way.
- Stick to your guns. Be consistent with your rules and make sure that others who look after your child do the same. Stick to punishments you impose – even if it makes you miserable.
- Say to the child 'This is unacceptable behaviour, we do not hit Fred/ bite Jemima', etc. Say that they will be punished if they continue the unacceptable behaviour. Always use the same format of words.

- Remember that a lot of what seems like bad behaviour is rooted in anxiety – can you work out what might be making them anxious? Is there a medical reason such as toothache or a headache?
- Listen to your child – when they are upset they may be trying to tell you something. See if there is a pattern to their behaviour.
- Don't move the boundaries – it will make them feel unsafe.
- Be prepared for it to take a long time to modify habits.
- Be sure that the child understands what they have done wrong, but remember that they are not very likely to learn from experience. You have to go over and over again how **not** to do something. Matt would promise that he would not do things again, but if someone said 'Try this', he always would.
- Remember that you are their safety net when they are in a tantrum; you provide the boundaries that make them feel secure.
- Keep your voice low and calm – go into a different room to scream!

To punish or not to punish?

All punishment has to be done as soon as the child has misbehaved or they will not know why they are being punished. Keep explaining again and again why you are doing this. Say 'Well done' when they have completed the punishment, so they get a better understanding that the punishment has finished and it is time to move on.

- As an effective method of punishment I would take away something Matt valued for a short time. I put the egg timer on to show how long the punishment was for, so that he could see it was not forever.
- With some older children, grounding can be effective, but you have to explain how it works each time you do this, and why you are grounding them.

Preventing dangerous or bad behaviour

If your ASD child is doing something dangerous and you have to stop them quickly, getting cross doesn't help. You can shout and it won't have any effect because they can't see why you are getting cross. They don't understand the dangers we see. I learned through Matt that what you have to do is explain over and over again why things are dangerous. For instance, with a fire, you show them pictures of some of the bad things that could happen, and that helps them to understand. ASD children still find the concept of cause and effect very hard to grasp, and you have to go over and over and over what may happen if they do whatever it is.

- Try to understand why the child is behaving this way – has something triggered the situation? Can you remove it or make it easier for next time?
- Remember that it is very likely that these children are working very hard to keep a lid on all their feelings during the school day, so by the time they get home they are just about ready to explode. You have to understand the level of stress they are coping with.
- Ask yourself if their anxiety levels are high and, if so, why?
- If you can find out what is making them unhappy, you will see why they are behaving badly.
- If their behaviour is dangerous, explain why they cannot do this, and, if you can, show them what the outcome could be.
- Channel them into something different.
- Talk to them about what makes them cross – remove it if you can, or try between you to find an acceptable way round it. Matt would wind people up because he liked to see their faces go red when he did. Accepting authority is hard for these children; they can't see why adults should tell children what to do, and yet they need the safety of discipline and structure.

Helping them to calm down

If the child is trying to do an activity and is getting anxious about it, then change how you do the activity. If the child is anxious because of something in the room, remove the child for five to ten minutes as a break. This should happen at your command. So you are saying 'Let's do something else' and then you can bring them back at the point where their anxiety levels have gone down and you can start again.

If they lose it totally they need to let off steam, so let them. Then go in and in a calm, low voice say 'Five, four, three, two, one, time out.' Then they have time out in a room where they can be quiet. You have helped them get over the anxiety and move on. You are the safety net. But, of course, you aren't always there. And it is important that they have some things they can do for themselves.

Teaching them how to calm themselves down

I taught Matt that if a teacher, or someone else, was shouting and he didn't like it, he should imagine the words just floating right over his head. He still finds that really helpful.

Sometimes at school Matt would put his hand up and say 'I need time out' and this kind of awareness, which comes before an anxiety state or tantrum can set in, is what we are aiming for.

Matt used to hold all his tension in all day at school and smile and get through the day and then explode when he got home. Some children will explode like this just anywhere, depending on the severity of their condition. Matt always seemed to know instinctively how to hold his feelings in until he got home – most of the time at least. He would be anxious as soon as I picked him up from school – you could see it in his body – and as soon as he got home he would keep saying 'time out'. He had to be left alone in his room for two hours and then he would come out and have tea and be fine. If he got interrupted, he would just explode and trash his room. He would smash a toy that he loved and at first he wouldn't make the connection that his rage had broken it and it would have to be thrown out – and he hated throwing things away. Matt learned to control those feelings himself, where it used to be me saying 'You need time out' and taking him to his room. We had to respect his need for time out. It was his safety net.

He had a 'time out' card at school, too, because otherwise he might throw a chair or something. If he got into a state where he could not cope in class, he got the card and the teacher let him go off to the special needs teacher's room, where he had a soft drink, calmed himself down and talked it through. Then we were able to analyse what triggered it – if the work was too hard, or there was something he didn't understand. Whatever it was, we were able to use the information for next time. It removed him from doing what he didn't want to do. Teachers are generally good about this kind of arrangement in my experience – better a 'time out' card than a table in your face.

We got Matt his own headset, which really helped. His anxiety would build up when there was a lot of noise around and so it helped when he could listen to music on the headset to block out everything around him for a while – which reduced his anxiety levels and it was something he could initiate for himself when it all got too much.

- Find some techniques that work for your child – like imagining anger-inducing words floating over their head.
- Give them a 'time out' space at home and respect their need for it.
- Get their teacher to let them have a 'time out' card at school – and make sure the teacher understands that when it appears they must take it seriously.
- Listening to music on a headset can block out noise that they are finding too much and help them to calm down.

> ### Getting cross by Matthew Keith Brealy, 14
>
> *'I get frustrated when teachers or people don't believe me this gets me cross, I hate it when people talk too fast I get lost in what they are saying. This gets me cross too. I don't like it when I get pushed I want to hit them when they do this I say stop it. My Mum has shown me that when people shout to let the words go over my head I feel this works and helps to control my anger.'*

Tips on temper control as they get older

As these children turn into young adults, I really believe that using the techniques in the book will pay off. I am not saying Matt or others I have taught do not lose their tempers, but they have found using the techniques helpful to them. Matt would still lose his temper but would go off of his own choice to cool down and then return. I would use that time to think of a way round his problem and then help him to put it into practice.

I did **not** do it for him, but with him. By doing the same, you will teach your child a new way to deal with difficulties and that they have to sort things out for themselves. You will also have helped them to realise that they can do things for themselves, and that is very empowering.

If you have a child or teenager who cannot sort things out for themselves then do it with them step by step.

- Let them cool off.
- Give them time out away from the situation at this point.
- Let them shout (we all do if we are not happy).
- Show them how to do whatever it is that has made them cross or frustrated.
- Do it with them if they struggle – slowly, or they will get even more frustrated.

Other people's intervention

Eddie's mum, Lesley, has found that other people struggle to know how to act with her son:

'When your child is having a meltdown quite a lot of what other people try to do makes it worse. Talking too much, too loudly and in their face really doesn't help. They don't realise that they won't get anywhere until the child has calmed down.'

Temper Control by Matt Brealy, 24

'I feel a little time to yourself normally sorts it out. If I'm at home I'll just switch my deck on. Music helps to chill me out you just need to find your own way to deal with anger. It's different for everybody isn't it?'

Waiting until everything has calmed down

Kate, Jack's mum, feels that things are improving as Jack grows up:

'Now that Jack understands himself better, he behaves better. There is no point in trying to hold a conversation when they are in a temper. Best to wait until they have calmed down. I agree with Jack in order to calm him down. I say things like "I can see why that makes you angry/I understand how you feel/I am on your side". When his feelings get bottled up it can lead to an explosion and that helps him release them. He doesn't swear or get abusive but he can shout. If Asperger's children are angry, they will say anything to hurt you – it doesn't mean anything and you have to understand that.'

8

Changes and obsessions – trying to achieve flexibility of thought

Matthew's major obsession when he was younger was lining up his cars and Action Men, which is a fairly textbook piece of behaviour. He would spend hours setting everything up and it had to be in exactly the right place. If I moved anything so much as a fraction he would notice in an instant and get very anxious. Among ASD children anxiety and panic attacks when we disrupt a pattern, or do something they don't understand, can cause behaviour that to an outsider looks like a violent tantrum, but in reality is anxiety that has gone off the scale.

When he was younger, Matt simply couldn't bear any deviation from routine and I realised that, for his own sake, we had to help him accept changes. Gradually, I started to make little changes to see how he would cope with them. I would put one of his toy cars round the wrong way and then I would say 'I like it that way round.' Then we would change another one together, and slowly he got the hang of changing things around. Then we took a really deep breath and repainted his room a different colour. Little by little he got used to changes like this and realised that they wouldn't hurt him.

Ways to achieve flexibility of thought

The rigid clinging to routine is a big part of ASD, and can cause your child lots of extra problems in coping with a world that does not always oblige by sticking to patterns. You can really help if you encourage them to see that little things in their day can change without anything terrible happening. Show them the positive side – for instance, they do not have to bath at 8 p.m. sharp every day, they can finish watching their television programme first if they want to.

You really have to help them to learn flexibility of thought. For instance, if you need to change something little, let the child help. Explain what needs to happen and ask how they think it can be done. Do not do this unless your child can cope with it – you will know from them when the time is right. I was overjoyed when, one day, Matt volunteered that I should pick his sister up before him, which was a change to routine that really helped me out on that day. He coped with it really well, partly because it had been his idea. It may seem like a small thing, but for us it represented a massive step forward in Matt's way of thinking.

When something needed to change in our daily routine, I would tell Matt what the change was and why it was going to happen and what was going to happen instead, and go over it lots of times. Then, just before the change happened, I would explain yet again. I know this seems incredibly long-winded but it is better than coping with a tantrum.

- Getting used to lots of insignificant little changes will help your child to feel safer with the idea of change.
- Explain any change in routine to them lots of times before it happens.

An adult perspective on obsessions

Here is a quote from an adult with Asperger's about her obsessions, which may help you to understand the way your child's mind is working:

'Sometimes things just have to be a certain way. It's hard to explain. If someone is phobic about snakes or spiders and you ask them to touch one that's completely harmless, they just can't do it. They know they're not being rational, but they simply can't overcome the block in their mind. If I need something to be a certain way, that's how I need it to be. If it isn't, I simply can't settle, can't sleep, will get up in the night to go and turn round an object I know is sitting askew on the kitchen shelf, for example. My way of dealing with this is to allow myself these compulsions if they don't interfere with my life, or with other people. Otherwise, I have learned to recognise the very start of a habit, and to nip it in the bud if I sense it will turn into an impractical compulsion. I say firmly to myself, "No! Don't be silly. You can't be having to walk clockwise round the table every time you need to put something on it," or whatever it is. Then I'll deliberately walk round the table anticlockwise.'

Obsessive interests

Matt had a bit of an obsession with fires. It started, rather unfortunately, when a teacher asked him to find out the difference between flammable and inflammable for homework. Matt wasn't to know that it was a trick question and, predictably enough, took a very literal approach to his research. Once we had cleared up the mess in the kitchen, it became his great interest to continue this research long term, and he discovered that quite a lot of things are, actually, flammable (or indeed, inflammable). It was quite hard to get him to stop but, as we clearly had to get through to him before he burned the house down, I discovered that you can get a fireman to come to your home and explain the unwisdom of starting little experimental fires around the place. A fireman in full uniform is an impressive sight, and Matt took his message very much to heart. If you are having problems with an obsession, it is worth looking for a simple and direct solution like this one.

Advantages of obsession

Jack's mum, Kate, explains that for Jack, obsessive concentration has some distinct advantages:

'When Jack was younger he was passionate about Lego™, and age six he could play with it for six hours straight, doing experiments on what you could do with the motor in his kit. Not a typical six-year-old, but classic Asperger's, and if it is not a benefit I don't know what is. Now at age 17 Jack has designed a typeface – being him it is not just 26 letters but a total of 590 symbols to make it complete. That fierce concentration is a very Asperger's trait.'

Matt's obsessions have changed over the years, and he has coped very well with keeping them at an acceptable level. He still likes everything to be in order – his clothes have to be put in the right drawers, for example. Getting used to small changes helped to make it easier for him to cope with big changes, using the same techniques as when he was younger, and made him better able to understand about things we can change and things we can't.

- As a parent you must choose your battles over obsessions with ASD youngsters. With some things you need to think about whether it really matters. For instance, if they like something in their room a particular way, well, we are all allowed our preferences sometimes.

Computers

If your child is an obsessive type, it's crucial you keep a watchful eye when it comes to computers. They can get obsessed with computer games and you need to be sure that they don't manipulate the time they spend on the computer. It can become their world so they don't socialise with the family. It's important to make a rule about the amounts of computer time and family time they must have.

Controlling screen time

Jack's mum, Kate, had to put rules in place to limit the amount of screen time Jack had.

'I was always very strict about computer time at home. Jack would argue the point, but he was always one to do what he was told (despite

arguing). He was obedient but very grouchy and would moan and moan about a rule. He argued about screen time rules but I always enforced them and he was not allowed a computer in his bedroom until he was 14. By then when he was on the computer he was not playing games but doing things like designing apps. At that age screen time really encroached on family time so then I had to control it. Mealtimes were important, but when he was stressed he found it hard to be around his squabbly brothers at mealtimes. So although I mostly enforced them for a while we did agree a three-meal-a-week opt out. Now he has resolved those stresses for himself.'

Learning to throw things away

ASD people tend to be collectors and don't like changing things by getting rid of anything. This is a life-long characteristic and dealing with it is an important part of conforming to normal life. Potentially, you could end up with a house crammed with stuff. I knew one person who found it hard to get rid of the wrappers off her food – imagine the smell. Every time you threw something away the anxiety of someone like that would be enormous, so you need to address the problem as early as possible. With something like food containers, perhaps you could try washing them and making models out of them for a while and then getting rid of them. It is all part of getting ASD children used to things they don't like.

Matt has had a big problem with throwing things away which I did a lot of work on. At one point we went through his wardrobe together and found things that were too small and that he didn't wear anymore, so we put them in a big bag to take to the charity shop. The idea that they weren't going to be thrown out but handed on to someone who might need them seemed ok with him, thus getting him used to the idea of recycling. It was important, so that when he had somewhere of his own one day it wouldn't be floor to ceiling with old shoes.

Transition

As we know, change of any kind is extremely hard for ASD children to cope with. When you know a change is coming up it will make things much easier if you do everything you can to ease the period of transition. Moving school, changing carers, moving house or any other major change is a very anxious time for ASD sufferers of any age. There is a lot we can do to help with this one, and I advise you do it!

- If moving school, ask if your child could do some extra familiarisation days in the school the week before they start. This will break them in slowly without the huge number of children starting on the same day and gives them the advantage of getting to know their way around the school a bit before the others arrive.
- Ask if you can both meet the new teacher together.
- Ask if you could have photos of the teachers who will be teaching your child. Take the pictures home and let the child get used to their faces. Remember to put the teachers' names at the bottom of each picture for an extra bit of familiarisation.
- Go over the route to school if it is new, using a map if you need to.
- Use a calendar to make a countdown to the day when school will start.
- If changing to a new carer, get a picture of him or her and cross the days off on the calendar till the old carer will leave and the new one will start.
- When moving house, take the child to the house to see all the rooms and to explore the new place.
- Count down to the move date.
- Show the child their new room.
- Show the child the route to the new house.

Make yourself some notes on how you dealt with any particular change; what helped and what didn't. You will find the notes really useful to refer back to next time a similar situation arises.

Bereavement and loss

A person with ASD will encounter many losses in their time, as for them the loss of a pen or a favourite item may well have equivalent significance to the loss of a person. You need to be ready for this and talk to them about replacing the lost item, which, ideally, they should choose. In the case of bereavement of a person you will need to have a long talk and explain the individual situation. When a person they are involved with in everyday life, such as a carer, is leaving, do the countdowns and charts described above. This prevents your child from having a huge build-up of anxiety and, once again, you are preparing them for a change, which they would find it hard to cope with unaided.

The new part of this section is a hard one for me as, since writing the first book, I have lost my son Paul. He was a passenger in a car crash and tragically died.

Being a close family this was a very big blow to us, but one thing is outstanding. Matthew was the one that held us together. All this time we have been helping him, and, in our hour of need, he stepped up. He helped us through a very bad time – I really don't know how we would have coped without him.

The day we heard the news Matt was working with his dad, and when the police told us he held us both in his arms and helped us through the terrible shock. When Paul was in the funeral place Matt came in with us. He was amazing and he helped us see things from a different point of view. I was devastated then Matt grabbed Paul's toe and said 'Ha ha, you can't get me back now.' It was a game they had always shared from boyhood, and he did it one last time. I just looked at him and with one of his big smiles he said 'Don't worry Mum, this is just his shell, our Paul is not there anymore. He is in the spirit world now,' which shocked me as I did not think that Matt would believe in that as you can't see it.

Matt picked us up when we were at our lowest. He even found little ways to help us through the day of the funeral. He did little things he knew his brother would like – put his hair right and put a rolled up cigarette behind his ear. He stood up and read a poem for his brother, and didn't find it hard to do at all. He showed a lot of compassion that people with Asperger's are not really supposed to have.

Losing Paul by Matt Brealy, 24

'When Paul died I think my Asperger's frame of mind may have made it easier to cope. You can't alter things like that – and people are dying every day. It was a big shock for everyone, but I was more able to think "What has happened has happened, it is a fact, accept the fact." It changed my outlook though; everyone should make the most of every day. Grief is so different for everyone. I dealt with it really well but seeing the effects of it on my parents was hard. We all have our different verdicts on death and after life, as I said to Mum and Dad it's just your body and your soul isn't there. I look at your body as being a trademark of you but your soul is elsewhere.'

Coping with bereavement

Kate, Asperger's mother of an Asperger's son on coping with a serious bereavement:

'I think ASD gives us an ability to detach when we have to. Both Jack and I have been much more closed with our emotions in bereavement than other close family, and that's the ASD. It doesn't mean we don't feel it – just that we don't show it.'

It may be possible to access a bereavement counsellor who has an understanding of specific ASD issues through the NAS autism helpline (0808 800 4104; www.autism.org.uk/enquiry).

Some tips on dealing with bereavement

- It is true that we avoid discussing death in families when we don't have to, but unexplained things are scary for ASD children so it is better to talk about the situation so that they can get used to things if possible. So explain, for instance, why Granny is going to hospital a lot, or why Grandpa is getting very thin.
- If it is possible, get your child used to the idea that someone close is going to die, and what that actually means, talking about it in a simple and straightforward way and using clear and unambiguous words. When you try, you will realise how much of what we say on this subject is cloudy – 'passing away', 'at rest' . . . this may comfort most of us but will just confuse your ASD child. You have to say they have died so that they are completely clear that the person in question will not be coming back.
- You shouldn't hide it from them when someone dies. Take them to the hospital or hospice and get them used to it.
- Be careful that you are not telling them that you have to be old to die. They need to be aware that although this very natural thing usually happens when you are older it can happen to someone young, and it can happen in a way that is not natural, so that they do not have an overwhelming shock in that sad situation.
- Use insects, plants or animals to discuss death as part of the natural life cycle – but prepare them, too, for lives cut unnaturally short. Looking at nature 'red in tooth and claw' can help you there.
- Make sure you keep their normal routine going as much as you can.

- ASD people may show their grief in ways that seem odd – obsession, clinging to routines, challenging behaviour. And reactions can be delayed – so be prepared.
- They may not seem to be upset – but if they are behaving in a way that is different to normal that indicates that actually they are.
- They can be confused because they don't see the person who has died any more, and you may have to explain this quite a few times.
- Seeing other people upset can make them anxious, and you need to be aware of this.

9

Strategies for dealing with day-to-day difficulties

Your ASD child sees most things in a different way to the rest of the family and, if left to themself – well, there is no point going down that road because, however much some of them might like it, they probably couldn't really be left to themselves. So, you have to fit everybody together so that life can run along reasonable lines. Nobody said it would be easy – but there are ways of dealing with a lot of daily challenges.

- Don't look for a miracle cure – work realistically to deal with what you have.
- Keeping a written record helps you to see patterns of behaviour.
- Filming behaviour on your phone or a camcorder can help. It is easier to understand what causes particular situations when you look at them from a calm distance and then you can deal with them.
- Look for a strategy in each situation.
- See if you are eligible for any grants that will help you to modify your house so that you can cope better.
- Respect your child's routines and need for sameness – for instance at bedtime.
- Doing things the way they like will really help them, so if you want to change something do it carefully.
- Adapting to their needs makes your life easier.

Sleep problems

When Matt was very young he didn't sleep and he was in and out of bed many, many times a night. That is very typical behaviour for ASD children. They don't seem to settle, they can't switch off and they quite often suffer from night terrors; scary, waking type dreams which are as disturbing for onlookers as they are for the sufferer. Matt would dream of things that he thought were really there – often it was snakes on the floor. At first we didn't know what to make of it. He was petrified. I would sit down and talk to him and calm him down. Sometimes we would have a hot drink and then we would go back and try to go to sleep again.

Taking our time seemed to work better than just putting the light on to show him there was nothing there and then going back to sleep. If we did that, a few minutes later he would be up again with the same thing. He needed us to spend that time with him to reassure him that everything was all right, and then get him back to sleep. If you put more time in yourself, you are more likely to get longer to sleep.

We actually did a video of Matt at night once to show the paediatrician how bad it was, and that was when he diagnosed night terrors. The camcorder helped us to look at the problem in the light of day and get some idea of how to deal with it.

That approach helped with all sorts of things with Matt's behaviour. I have always tried to look at what he was doing and write it all down. Being slightly removed from a situation helps you to see it more clearly and I found it was often easier to see why he was acting in a particular way when I thought about it later.

If you are tired at night, the last thing you want is to start thinking about what to do, but if you already have a plan in place it really helps in the middle of the night. That is not the time for strategy forming. Camcording, taking notes and watching helped us to understand what was going on and to make a plan. Matt still got the terrors from time to time and when this happened we took our time over the routine of going in, turning the light on, showing him there was nothing there and encouraging him to go back to sleep.

We came to understand that if Matt's anxiety was raised in the day, we might have terrors in the night – it is all about unfinished business. He would shout and scream and walk about touching things. In the morning he had no idea what had happened. He was tired, but he had no idea why. Bits of what he remembered from his dream would come out in conversation during the day. We tried to talk to him about the night terrors but he never remembered anything. He might have been up wandering around all night, but as far as he was concerned he was in bed asleep. It could be a big problem for the family, and if your child suffers in this way it may help to adopt a few of these strategies.

Strategy for winding down in the evening

- Start calming your child down at least an hour before bed so they have time to unwind.
- Try using lavender oil in the room if they like it; this has a calming effect.
- Hot milky drinks work for some.
- Watch a calming favourite DVD, read a story, play together calmly with a favourite toy.
- Do all of these things together unless your child is happier alone. If you are together then you can check they are calming down.

Matt used to disturb the others. All three boys were in a bedroom together and the other two couldn't sleep through his night terrors, so were really tired for school the next morning. Sometimes he would do things like getting out of bed and hitting them with toys, pulling their duvets off, swapping things from bed to bed, moving things around. The upshot was that they just weren't sleeping and we were ending up with three grumpy boys in the morning instead of just one.

It was going from bad to worse, so, when I found out that I could get a grant towards getting another bedroom built in the attic, we were overjoyed. The older boys were able to move upstairs, where they could get their sleep undisturbed, and Matt moved into the small room next to us so that we could keep an eye on him.

Bedtime was always a problem for Matt. We would put him to bed and he would be in and out sometimes till 11 or 12 at night, sometimes later, and then we were up I don't know how many times in the night. With bedtime we always had to stick to exactly the same routine. We had to check the windows, the curtains, under the bed, the duvet cover had to be right, the sheet had to be right. We found it better that one of us did it rather than both, so my husband made the routine where he went in every single night. Matt settled much more quickly if everything was right. We had to have a respect for what he needed, and this was central to our approach.

In some houses they might have started saying 'This is ridiculous at his age' and tried to make him conform to a more normal pattern, but we felt that respecting him as him was a key to helping him. Our long-term aim was always that Matt would like to be able to put himself to bed, and we worked towards it bit by bit, doing one less thing for him every so often until he had conquered that part of the routine for himself. It took about 12 to 18 months for Matt to achieve independence in this area; by age 11 he was more or less ok.

- Doing things the way ASD children like them is an important way to help them, so if you do need to change something do it very carefully.

Matt used to get very anxious if I so much as changed his duvet cover, because he always looked at the pattern when he was going to sleep and having the same shape, colour and pattern was very important to him. We got him to choose his own duvet covers so that he could make sure that they had a pattern he was comfortable with. By adapting to his needs we made our own lives easier as well.

When we went on holiday, sleep was an issue for him and he was worried. He actually wanted to dismantle his bed and take it with us, so we took his duvet instead, which made him feel secure and relaxed once we had made him understand that we had no room to take the whole bed. Then he felt settled because, with his duvet on the holiday bed, it looked like his bed at home. The look of things, the shapes, the patterns are very important to people with ASD.

Matt used to get up early and roam around the house but then he settled into a more teenage routine and stayed in bed for hours if he got the chance. We got used to the early start, it was just part of his pattern. The house was as safe as we could make it and we kept our door open so we could hear him, though nine times out of ten we would probably get up with him anyway. That didn't worry me nearly as much as keeping the night terrors at bay.

For a long time Matt would pop in to talk to his sister in the night or come in to us, pull the curtains back in the middle of the night and describe the clouds and the moon. He would offer to count the stars for us, but at two or three in the morning all we wanted was that he would go to sleep.

Medication – pros and cons

Some ASD children just can't switch off. Matt sometimes used to take a drug called Melatonin, a natural hormone supplement that has a role in sleep cycles. When it was originally prescribed we used it quite a lot to get him into the pattern of bed/sleep. Once we got the pattern established I withdrew it and then he only had it when he really needed it, which was when he was so wound up that he simply couldn't switch off. Matt still finds some nights he can't sleep. He uses relaxation techniques to help him unwind, but sleep can still be a big problem.

Jack, the boy I help, also had real problems to do with not being able to switch his brain off, and he would say 'My head keeps going buzz, buzz, buzz all the time and I can't turn it off.' He is getting better at knowing when he needs sleep as he gets older, and copes better when he can't, but the doctors never came up with much to help him.

I didn't use drugs for any other areas of behaviour with Matt. I have seen Ritalin work with other children and I have seen times when it has really helped, but I have also seen cases where it has made the child really dopey and not with it and, personally, I wanted Matt to be as much himself as possible. But then, he is a relatively mild case, and I would never think that parents should rule this out as a possibility. It is very much down to the individuals. I have seen cases where a child just can't slow down and Ritalin has made them much better.

Food problems

It was very apparent from a young age that whereas the others would eat anything, Matt wouldn't, and he didn't even want to try things. Foods he didn't like would make him gag. I didn't want him to end up with a food phobia, so from when he was about three I used to get him to help me cook and try, smell, feel, touch, taste everything while we were cooking, so that he knew all the way through what the food was going to be like. I used to let him sit on the worktop while I was preparing food and taste and play with anything. He would taste things that were safe to eat raw before they were cooked and then again after they had been cooked, so he was following the process right the way through. It meant that he could understand the food, rather than just being confronted with it at meal times.

When he helped me cook it he was so proud that he had helped, and dishing it up for Dad and his brothers made him really happy. It helped him a lot and got him over a lot of phobias. If you do the same with your ASD child, do take a picture of the meal that you have both prepared to add to your picture/word collection.

Eggs were a real problem for a long time. I showed Matt pictures of hens and eggs and things that you could cook with eggs to help him. They do have a slimy texture, which he hated, but he didn't mind eating eggs in cakes and things because then the texture had changed. I got eggs into his diet by cooking them in other things and it was a long time before he was able to eat them on their own.

When we went to the supermarket he would pick things up and smell them because that was how he identified food. He often didn't remember even foods we have regularly. If you asked if he would like a beefburger, which he has had hundreds of times, he would ask what it looked like so that he could think what it was.

I think cooking together was one of my biggest turnarounds with him and I am sure that it stopped an awful lot of fads with his food: by his teenage years he would eat around 90% of what was offered.

I did the same with drinks because of the different colours, which fascinated him. If I changed to a different colour of washing-up liquid he would have to taste it to see if it was the same because it looked different; even bleach and household cleaners got the same treatment if I wasn't careful. You name it, he would try it, even though I put things right away and then labelled them with a sick sign, meaning that they would make you sick if you tried them; he wasn't tasting things to be naughty, just in a spirit of enquiry.

Once the boys brought home tadpoles and he picked one up, looked at it, smelled it and then, before we could stop him, he ate it. He said that it was a bit slimy. Then he kept doing it every time one of the tadpoles changed shape because to him it was something different then. When supermarkets changed the wrapper on something, as far as he was concerned it was a new thing and had to be investigated all over again. When Matt was younger, every day was a new day for all the impressions that he got and each everyday thing that he saw was a new thing. He was always smelling and tasting things in the house and garden or at the shops, as a way of getting to know them.

- Get poor eaters to help you cook – they will lose their suspicion of food if they understand how it is put together and may find it more interesting if they have made it themselves. Different textures may become more acceptable this way, too.
- I worked with an autistic child who had a food phobia. I boiled up a load of spaghetti and put it on my nose, my head, throwing it and having a great time with it so he saw me being completely unafraid of it and having fun with it so he wanted to join in and have fun and after that he was not afraid of touching it. Gradually you could broaden something like that out to other foods.
- Incidentally, almost all the children I have dealt with have had digestive problems where they find it really hard to go to the loo in a normal way. How can a child with no speech tell you they are constipated? A lot of their distressed behaviour could come down to a cause as simple as this. Do watch out for this if you can't see anything else that might be causing a behaviour problem.

I have found that using the techniques in the book for getting used to food on Matt from a young age has really paid off. He will now try just about any food, including cooked bugs in Thailand!

> **Food by Matt Brealy, 24**
> *'I have overcome all the food issues from when I was young apart from the fact that I still don't like slimy food. I like cooking.'*

Difficulties with obesity

Emerging research suggests links between ASD and obesity, and, when you think about it, it is hardly surprising that eating can be an issue for ASD children. Overeating can become an obsession, or sometimes they just don't have a sense of when to stop. One thing you can do is to enforce a regime of rigid mealtimes and no snacks, otherwise children like this will just eat all day. Other ASD children actually have to be reminded to eat, or they can simply forget if left to themselves.

- If your child starts to find food a challenge, play with food and let them have fun with it so they are not afraid of it.
- Experiment with lots of food in groups so they see others tasting it too.
- Get your child to research healthy foods with you.
- Make up menus for the week's food together.
- Play some sports with your child, or join a gym together. If you don't like sport then enrol your child in a club – this might give you a bit of respite time and your child a bit of independence.
- If your child does not like lots of people around make a home gym, and use exercise DVDs and games. If you make the activities fun they will want to keep doing them.
- Make it a family thing to do keep fit and healthy eating.
- Let them help with the shopping. Showing them what is healthy makes them more aware, too.
- If your child has a high level of autism then take steps with the help of a nutritionist.

Timekeeping

We found that although Matt could tell the time, it didn't mean much to him. If I told him he needed to be in a certain place at a certain time he might try, but he was still easily distracted if he bumped into someone or something happened. He does understand the concept of lateness because as a teenager every time he was late, he found he wasn't allowed out the following night. When he lost something he wanted to do, it did register with him. I would tell him that if he was on time, he could go out again the following night. I couldn't say that Matt has ever really grasped the concept of being on time, but anyway here are some things that we have found helped a bit and could help you.

- Give your child a watch.
- Write the time you need them to be back on their hand.
- Let them have a mobile phone and make sure it is switched on.
- Try using a timer that goes off in their pocket.

These are all useful things to try. Matt still switches off the phone or timer then forgets that he is supposed to be somewhere or meeting someone.

Matt continues to find timekeeping hard, but he gets to work on time. When he is not at work he just relaxes with his timekeeping, but I do not think this is a problem as it his social life that it affects. If I need him to go somewhere, I tell him he needs to get there earlier than he does.

- In order to avoid the sensation of being rushed, which is super-stressful for people with ASD, give them plenty of time.

Being quick

ASD children can't rush, and you can't make them rush, because, if you do that, you are asking them to do too many things in one go: to think of the time, to get ready, to think about getting out of the door, all at once. And they will be very easily distracted.

- Egg timer – give a reward if the child beats the egg timer.
- Have a reward ready to give in the car if your child has been quick.

Remembering

Matt had a total lack of short-term memory. He could have something in his hand and I would say 'Go and put this in your bag in the next room' and he would forget before he got there.

- To help your child remember what they need for the day try making a laminated checklist (using either words or pictures) of items they need for school. Punch a hole in it and put it on a chain attached to their school bag. 'Have I got homework/reading book/sports kit/lunch box/coat?' With a list like this they can check for themselves and feel in control.

Matt will use his phone for this nowadays; they are great as you can do so much on them and no one takes any notice of you using your phone as it is a pretty normal thing to do.

Dressing

Here you will encounter the difficulties of an extremely literal approach to instructions – they will do **exactly** what you say, so you have to say **exactly** what you want them to do. I always reminded Matt what clothes to put on in the morning and in what order. When I walked past his room I gave the whole sequence of dressing instructions one thing at a time – right down to each sock and each shoe, and very gradually things improved. Once, when his father was getting him ready for school, he ended up setting off without his shoes because nobody had reminded him to put them on.

- Make a picture wall chart of the clothes they put on in the morning and a timetable of their routine, e.g. wash/dress/breakfast, and put it next to a clock on the wall to help with timing as well (if you are lucky!).

As they grow up they all of a sudden decide what they like to wear. They become individuals and it allows their personality to come through. Matt likes his clothes to be just right, and certainly has his own style.

Learning patience

Jamie's mum, Finni, found that patience was the main virtue involved in teaching her clever son how to deal with everyday life:

'For me personally, things got easier once I understood the difficulties and had the patience to realise that if I spent ages teaching him to tie up the laces on his gym shoes I would have to spend the same amount of time teaching him to tie up the laces on his school shoes because they were different shoes. There is no blueprint so everything has to be learned for the first time. In his world there are no received ideas at all. Once you have learned the patience involved with coping with that, it is not a problem.'

Out and about

You can give an instruction to an autistic child and have them parrot it back to you but if they can't connect what it means, they won't be able to put it into practice. For instance, I taught Matt the Green Cross Code, so he knew the words that told him that he had to stand at the kerb. But when I took him out into the road he couldn't relate the rhyme in his head to what he actually had to do. Saying the Green Cross Code aloud as you are doing it can help, but I found crossing the road the same way every time more help as it became routine. Matt would just go off if he saw something interesting, so I got a wrist-to-wrist attachment and used it for ages, and when he was too old for that he **had** to hold someone's hand when he was out or he would be off.

- If you have a real wanderer get a tracking device or one of those key rings that bleep, and attach it to their clothes when you go out so that you can find them and they know that you can find them.

Matt came to love to be out and about. All the hard work with the Green Cross Code paid off and he learned to properly understand cars and how the road system works. This took away all the stress that being around cars used to cause him. He still wandered off to look at things but it was easier when he was older and had an understanding of the roads. If your youngster cannot cope with this on their own then, when they are old enough, it might be nice to buddy them up with a companion of about the same age to help them go out and about and stay safe.

Travelling in the car

Another thing Matt did, which took me a long time to understand, was that if we travelled somewhere by car, he would suddenly start screaming and trying to get himself out of his seatbelt, while the others were trying to hold him in. He would be screaming that he 'needed England', sweating with nerves and flapping his arms. Once, we were on the dual carriageway and he tried to open the door to get out. At that point we had to change the car to one with doors at the back that he could not open. He knew that England was where he lived and where home was, but if I took a different route to normal, he thought that he was leaving England and losing everything familiar. He didn't like it if you changed routes or routines, because he always wanted everything to be the same. I had to spend a lot of time with him using a map to show him that the route would bring us back, and I showed him that the road on the map was called Wisteria Avenue and we were parked in Wisteria Avenue, so he could relate the map to what we were doing. Then he started saying things like 'This is just a different road, isn't it? We are going to the same place but just on a different road.'

- Photocopy a map and draw the road you take so the child can follow it and not get anxious. The next time you do that journey take a slightly different route with a different marking on the map. They can see that it all ends up in the same place so they can get used to changing routes and spare you all from some agitation.

If I took Matt into a multistorey car park at this time, he would just go berserk because there were cars pulling in, pulling out, going one way, going the other way and he couldn't keep his eyes on what was going on around him. I actually took him into car parks and sat in the car with him for a long time when he was little and let him watch the cars. It helped when I explained that if there was an arrow on the floor they had to go that way. Once he knew there was a structure and rules he turned a corner on that particular anxiety and we could go into multistorey car parks without him getting upset. He would remark on how many cars were there, but he had learned to cope with the anxiety of what was going on around him.

Thanks to what he learned about maps, Matt learned to go anywhere without worrying about getting back. He will work out his route and off he goes, and if the road is blocked or closed, he will have another look and go round it another way.

Matt had a moped when he was 16. Amazingly, guys like him do stick to the Highway Code and the rules of the road – they do love a rule. Now he is looking to do his driving test and, again, he likes the fact that there will be rules within the car, but is annoyed when other drivers break the rules. His improved understanding of others has helped here, but he still does not like the fact that they may not drive correctly.

Shopping

Have a list of foods you need and let your child help to look for them; this also helps with memory and recognition, and helps you to get your shopping done more quickly.

If your child does not like shopping, ask someone to look after them while you do the shopping; remember that those with ASD generally do not like places where there are a lot of people. Again, you are respecting them for who they are. You can get over this fear by slowly getting your child to help you do the shopping, by going to small shops first and working your way up to big stores.

- Have a list. It is quicker and will keep your child occupied.
- Explain to them why people do not like it when you smell the food on sale in shops, and go over this lots of times.
- Show them that no one else in the shop is doing this.
- Explain that you can leave the shop more quickly if they help.
- Most of all, reward them at the end of the shopping trip, perhaps by buying something they like to collect, such as a magazine or stickers, or a treat such as something to eat.

These days Matt loves cooking, so he has to be organised, know what is in the recipe and then shop for the food. He does not like it if the shop is busy but has learned to go when the shops are quiet.

Here are some useful tips for independent shopping.

- Do a menu for the week's meals.
- Write a shopping list – make a new one each week and only get what you need. Make sure you stick to the list.
- A recipe book is a great gift for ASD youngsters embarking on independent living. They will follow the instructions to the letter.
- Suggest that they shop at quiet times to avoid stress and distraction.

Holidays

We always went to the same place on holiday – the one time we went somewhere different it took Matt such ages to relax that none of us could really wind down.

- You can prepare your child for a holiday by using a map to show them the route you are going to use.
- Tell them all about what to expect when they get there.
- Take some familiar things with you to make them feel at home.

Matt has now discovered that he loves to visit other countries and enjoys planning his journeys. He travelled to Thailand and Vietnam, and his ability to use maps definitely helped with this. We made laminated lists of essential things like contact numbers and put them in a folder for him, and once he realised that everything he needed was in one accessible place he felt confident that he could manage ok.

> ## Travelling by Matt Brealy, 24
> *'I love travelling. Dad sorted me out a folder for the paperwork and I stick with that system. As long as you have everything organised it is not a problem. I managed to get six people from one end of Vietnam to the other without getting killed so I think my organisation is ok now. I travelled in Vietnam with some Canadian guys, so I would like to go to Canada next and then to South America.'*

Becoming independent

Matt's dad, Keith, felt that the independent travelling was one of Matt's greatest achievements:

'He did manage to save money to go travelling with his friends to Thailand and Vietnam, and really took control of their travelling arrangements and accommodation while they were away, which shocked us, but he said that because we were not with him he had to get on with it. Matty has always loved travelling and meeting different cultures, and I think this is something he will always do.'

10

Getting organised can save your sanity

You need to be very organised as a parent of an ASD child, especially when there are other children in the family, too. I have found that if you are disorganised, the household becomes very stressful to all and anxiety is not just the child's problem but yours, too!

To avoid this, look at all you do and make it your job to get it right. If you have an aim and purpose, you will find it easier; I know I do.

How to modify your home

Just look around and you will find lots of simple things you can do in your house that will make everyone's lives run more smoothly.

- Although a child with ASD is often pretty noisy, they can also be sensitive to noise. You can reduce noise levels in your house with carpets instead of wood or laminate flooring.
- Soft lighting is kinder than harsh fluorescent light.
- It can be helpful to ASD children if the furniture is around the edges of the room, with the middle space kept fairly clear.
- Patterns can be confusing and anxiety-inducing to walk or sit on, so keep carpets and furnishings as plain as you can.

- Duvets, beanbags and comfy chairs can help ASD children feel safer and calmer.
- Make sure your house is as safe as it can be. Foil escape artists wherever possible. ASD children have little sense of danger, so prepare for the unexpected. Have locks for windows and cupboards, and keep plug covers in use long term. An ASD child really never grows out of tinkering with things.
- One idea is to put bells on all your doors, with different chimes for different doors, so you know which room your child is going into, and can keep track of them around the house – or if they are trying to get out of the house.
- After the distressing incident when Matt cleaned his teeth with haemorrhoid cream instead of toothpaste, I locked all the medical stuff in a box on a high shelf in the bathroom that he couldn't reach, and we have kept it there ever since.
- Try to give them their own space to chill out and calm down when they need to. They need this as much as anyone else does, probably more.
- Somewhere to exercise and let off steam is brilliant. For instance, trampolines are often a great success.
- Check that you don't have anything poisonous in the house, and that includes plants.
- Pictures of objects to help the child understand what they have to do, such as get dressed in the morning, get ready for school, can be stuck in appropriate places around the house.

Think of it as your **job**. Ok, it's unpaid, but well worth it. You are your own boss, so you can make your own timetable of the day, one that works for you and the rest of the family. Keep to your timetable – it will help you and your family to get organised.

Be prepared for things to go wrong and work out how to deal with them if they do, so you can stay on track.

How to modify your life

- Make packed lunches the night before and make all your children pack their school bags the night before; make a timetable that takes problems into account.
- Be generous with your timing so you don't need to rush. If something goes wrong, you have time to spare so you won't have to get tense and worried about being late.

- Don't set your targets too high to start with. If you fail at something, you will feel bad about it and that is no good for you.
- If you want to go out in the morning, get things ready the night before. You can even pack the car up, then you don't have to rush.
- Lay the clothes out the night before, ready for your ASD child to put on in the morning; ask what they would like to wear to wherever you are going.

I used printed timetables to help me keep track of my observations with Matt and I found them really useful, so I have put in a couple as examples. You can ask for this to be done in school as well, which can help to pinpoint any daily difficulties, and helps with liaison between home and school.

Home

Date	Time	Target	Comments
10/7	7 a.m.	Get up	Still finds this hard – need to wake him slowly
10/7	7.15 a.m.	Have a wash	Remember to say each item: flannel, soap, wash face, etc.
10/7	7.30 a.m.	Get dressed	Needs help with buttons – need to practise more
10/7	7.45 a.m.	Have breakfast	Eat with a spoon – still need to practise
10/7	8.00 a.m.	Get in car	Needs more time

The timetable showed me that I needed more time to help Matt get out in the morning so I needed to wake the whole family up earlier.

School

Date	Time	Target	Comments
10/7	9.00 a.m.	Sit in registration	Sat for 3 mins. Need to work on sitting – use egg timer
10/7	9.15 a.m.	Do 4 sums in maths, then practical maths	Found this hard today, got 2 sums done then did practical maths. Next time I will go back to the last 2 sums
10/7	9.45 a.m.	Go over writing in English lesson	Finds hand-eye co-ordination hard

10/7	10.15 a.m.	Break time – try to sit and eat fruit with other children	Does not like to sit and eat with other children so I sat with him and encouraged him – keep it going

As you can see, it is very straightforward. It helps a lot as, if your child gets cross, it is all logged. This helps as a way to keep track of what progress your child is making at home or school.

Putting systems in place

Kate has found that the important thing is to help Jack to organise things for himself. Her strategies include an iron rule that certain things can only live in one place.

'In 18 months of school, for instance, Jack never lost his tie because he had to hang it up right by the door and so it was always in the same place. He has to have a strategy for stuff he can't do, for instance lists and checklists of what he took to school when he started secondary. I started by packing his bag, but made him check it, then he packed it and I checked it, then he was on his own with the occasional spot check from me. We did this in half-termly increments, which was plenty of time to get used to each stage.

'We needed systems for homework. He had a planner calendar where he could write down all the homeworks, and, crucially, when he had to hand them in, so he could see at a glance when the work was due. Things like the UCAS form are still a real struggle for him.

'We had lists pinned up by the door of things he needed to remember before he left the room. Now he has got good at finding his own ways to make him remember stuff.'

Smartphones, iPads and computers can be a blessing on the organisation front for ASD children, because they can have all the information they need for their day at school, for instance, all in one place in front of them. Although, of course, there is always the danger that a phone can easily be mislaid.

11

Schooling

Mainstream versus special schools

Deciding what kind of education is going to be best for your ASD child is one of the hardest decisions that you are going to have to make. There is a lot to be said in favour of both mainstream and special schooling, although in some areas lack of a decent choice means that the decision is virtually made for you. Parents faced with the dilemma of deciding what is best for their child often don't know all their rights in this area, and they may face a real battle.

Special schools provision is very limited in some areas and mainstream teachers need more specialised training and acceptance of their role. There is a need for more specialist attention in mainstream schools where some teachers still have scant understanding of the problems ASD children face.

Within the framework of what is available, the most important thing when you are making a decision is to base it on the character of your child and what is likely to be best for him or her. A child's intelligence level is nothing to do with whether they are within the spectrum or not, so your decision will not be made purely on academic grounds. Make a list of their needs and consider how each one will be met. Make a list of the important features of each way of educating and how they match up with your child's needs. For instance, sending a nervous, clingy child away to boarding school would probably be torture for you both, however good the facilities, although for a different type of child it might offer possibilities of independence or a level of care that would be entirely beneficial.

Making the right choice

Clare Ryan has three children on the autistic spectrum and knows that the right choice of school for each child is of paramount importance.

'A well-informed choice of school helps you, and also access to autistic adults who can explain how things feel. I was upset at the time of my son's diagnosis, not because I wanted to change him, but because I didn't want him to have to struggle. Parents need to deal with their own feelings fast and get over them so that they can get on with being the advocate/support for their children. Just getting a diagnosis letter is very bleak – there needs to be some support. I had a lot of help from Ambitious about Autism (www.ambitiousaboutautism.org.uk), the national charity for children and young people with autism, where you can get useful support and advice.

'I have done a total of five tribunals for my children's education and I know it was worth all the hard work I put in.'

Mainstream school – our choice for Matt and how we made it

We chose to send Matt to the same local school that his brothers attended. I wanted him to follow the lead of ordinary children and I felt that it was important for him to develop his social skills. That did influence my decision to go for mainstream school.

I didn't think Matt was independent enough to go away from home to special school, as a boarding school was the only option available to us, and I also felt that as a parent I would be letting him down if I sent him away. I didn't want someone else to take over things I felt I should be doing myself.

If there had been a special day school that could have offered Matt what he needed, my decision might have changed. Some children might well be happier in an environment where they do not feel so different, such as a special school where everyone is like them. I felt that it would cut down on Matt's chances to assimilate into the real world and to experience life, even if he was led a bit of a dance by some of his friends at mainstream school.

One negative aspect of mainstream schooling is that not all the teachers understand or appreciate the difficulties of an ASD child. I think the parent-teacher relationship is difficult with special needs. You have to be able to feel sure that they want the best for your child and there needs to be considerable understanding and support on both sides. As a trained special needs learning support assistant who is also a parent of an ASD child, I hope I have more compassion than is often the case.

As a parent you have to let the teachers do their job, although that can be hard. One thing you can do is give the teachers a folder with all the relevant information on how you talk to and discipline your child, things that you feel would be helpful when they are dealing with your child.

With the policy of inclusion in primary schools there is far more chance for the other children to assimilate understanding of differences without really being aware. Having a physical disability is easier for them to see and understand than a disability like Matt's, where people can look and talk normally but then behave inappropriately. Children pick it up much more quickly than adults, but some handle it better than others. I wanted Matt to be able to be himself and for everyone to accept him for who he is.

Tips for the transition to secondary school

Making the transition from mainstream junior to secondary school can be traumatic for any child, for an ASD child much more so. Both schools need to be involved to make the change as successful as possible.

- It helps if you can organise familiarisation visits beforehand, make a map of the school and get pictures of the relevant staff for your child to get used to.
- Let the school know about your child's likes and dislikes and any things that might upset them.
- As a parent, be open to suggestions and ideas – keep an open mind and keep up to date with new strategies and ideas. Both sides – parents and school – should be receptive to suggestions.
- Make sure your child and the secondary school are both ready for the transition. Have things in place and know what is in store. Make sure that ways to deal with potentially stressful situations are covered on both sides.
- Make sure you have a good line of communication with the school – someone you can get in touch with such as the SENCO, head of year or form teacher.

- ASD children may well not be keen on a big noisy dining hall. If asked, the school may provide, or have already, a quiet room for packed lunch/ supervised games/help with homework, where an ASD child can feel safe and away from social situations that they might find difficult.

Other options to consider

Of course there are lots of other educational choices to bear in mind, and I thought the best way of looking at them was to talk to people involved in different areas to find out the good – and the bad – points that might help you with a decision.

Special school

There is enormous pressure on special school places in most parts of the country, so Lesley Burton felt that she was very lucky to get a place at a local state special school for her son, Eddie.

'Because we got our diagnosis early we were advised to get Eddie a place at our borough's flagship special school which is not too far from home. He was happy there to start with at age three but as the years went by we had major questions about how suitable it was for his secondary education. We felt that the education was not autism specific, though it is the recommended school within the borough. It deals with a number of different disabilities and only had a certain allocation for speech therapy and there was often none available for him as there were many other children with more serious and urgent needs. It really wasn't meeting Eddie's needs but there are massive difficulties in moving from the borough's own special needs school to another special needs school. It was a battle and we had to get a specialist advocate to help us. We got Eddie assessed by an educational psychologist assessor. When he first went to the school Eddie was MLD (moderate learning difficulties) and during his time there he had slipped to SLD (severe learning difficulties) and the school could not help him back though it was felt that he had the potential. They were really holding him back.

'We got him assessed at Hillingdon Manor, a flourishing independent specialist school for children on the autistic spectrum, which was set up in 1999 by Anna Kennedy, when her two autistic sons were turned away by 25 mainstream schools. The assessment indicated that Eddie had a lot of potential and they thought he would fare best in a class where the curriculum

was pitched at a level that would challenge him. We moved him to the school and he has never looked back. It is exactly the right school for him, though I know that it is not for everyone.

'Eddie's speech and language therapies and day-to-day life are totally embedded in the school. He can now say loads, he has eye contact, he is reading and he is a star for maths. His cognitive ability is fantastic though his communication is very poor and he has a bit of verbal dyspraxia as well, so when he does speak it sounds a bit strange. But from being completely non-verbal this represents massive and very welcome progress.

'His self-esteem has soared because he has been able to achieve so much more in a variety of things. He does sports, music, and woodwork. They take all the children out to a restaurant every week and he tries using words and pictures and his iPad to communicate what he wants. He pays for his own food. It is all about communicating in an appropriate way and is a great way to enhance independence and communication skills. His previous school just couldn't deal with his individual needs and we are so grateful that we were able to make the change. He can stay till he is 18 – he is 13 now with a mental age of four to five in some respects.

'This is a golden time for Eddie. He loves school, he loves his activities, he loves his teachers, and he is secure and happy at home with all his family. He and his siblings all get along beautifully. He brings out their caring side. He will do anything that his little sister says, and she often takes care of him. We have found the right school for him, and I would say to any parent that if you can identify what is the right thing for your child it is worth fighting to get it. We were lucky that our borough did listen to us and I know that this doesn't always happen, so you need to enlist all the backup you can. If you have choices, make sure that you have all the facts you can muster.'

The compromise solution – introducing special needs into the mainstream

Some special schools have an innovative approach to inclusion whereby children with special needs are taken from the special school into a mainstream school for some lessons or activities. Children who go to the special school get specialist input from experienced and knowledgeable teachers and they can go in and out of mainstream school for the subjects they can manage or even just for social inclusion. This way these children have the best of both worlds. They really benefit from the stimulation at the mainstream school and can be stretched in their good subjects, which they might not get at their special school. At the same time, being at the top of the group at special school does wonders for their self-esteem, whereas, if they were full-time in mainstream, they might sink.

Alexander Lubbock attended a Chinnor unit, within a state school. These are self-contained units in several Oxfordshire schools, which allow pupils to integrate into main school classes where it is beneficial. His father, John Lubbock, is pleased with the merits of this type of structure.

'You can go right through school as an autistic child in the system. The unit is brilliant, completely self-contained and almost one-to-one staff, and the children can go out into the school for whatever they can manage. Some don't go at all, some go a lot. Alexander is a very clever boy but he is quite severely autistic. We felt that at this stage it was better for him to be out in the world than not. He did PE and drama in the main school and joined them for lunch and play. He pretty much ignored everybody, but was happy to be there and proud to be in a proper school. His primary school was a Chinnor unit on this model as well: we felt very lucky to live in a place where this is available.'

The academic mainstream – problems for a high achieving Asperger's sufferer

Finni Golden's son, Jamie, is highly academic, but as someone with mild Asperger's, life at school had its problems for him.

'Jamie has the normal problems associated with Asperger's in his social life, but not particularly in his educational life. He is very intelligent – he understands concepts and is very clear thinking. He is clever, conscientious and hardworking but he is driven by a terrible perfectionism and he suffers terribly with OCDs, which are his nightmare. Part of that has a good result in that he likes to get everything finished and it has to be done perfectly, so I never had to stand over him with a stick to get homework done. As with a lot of these conditions you do have to find and respect the positive.

'A special school would probably never have been a suitable option but mainstream school is particularly difficult for children like him who

are generally not good at any sport because they often have motor problems with co-ordination and so on. Jamie got teased for being an egghead and a nerd and all those awful things that children taunt each other with. He is quite hot-headed as well, which I think goes with the general anger at being different, so he would sometimes retaliate to his own detriment.

'It takes him a long time to settle anywhere and he was unhappy at his school for quite a while. The best advice I could give to someone in a similar situation is persevere where you are if you can, because it doesn't actually matter which school you put them in, they are initially going to have a very difficult time with some of the other children. Jamie always had problems in that he was probably three years younger than his age socially and three years older academically. He learned to read when he was two and was keen to know about everything. He demanded to know what letters and symbols meant almost before he could speak. At prep school he found it very hard before the diagnosis of Asperger's and I just thought I had a very bright and difficult child.

'His teachers were generally sympathetic, but whether they did anything positive to help him is another matter. It became easier for him as he got older because, in education generally, there is much more awareness of the problems these days and they have things in place including a specific member of staff to help with special learning difficulties.

'At the gifted end of the spectrum, mainstream education is something my son coped with, but it has not been easy by any stretch of the imagination. Academically able children have a different set of problems. They need to be stretched by their education, otherwise it is very frustrating for someone clever.'

Home education

Although home education is sometimes a first choice, it is often a response to problems with mainstream education. This was certainly the case for Elaine Holyer, who felt very strongly that her son James was at a school that was unable to meet his special needs.

After years of battling to get a statement and then battling to get the school to keep to the provisions of it – after all it is a document of law – I felt very let down by the system. I was told that our area is known not to be a good provider of special needs education, but that is really no comfort at all.

'I am very pleased with our decision to home educate. I don't think that James had really learned anything in his two years at secondary school. Help was just not geared towards him. I had to fight to get him a teaching assistant and, as she was previously a lollipop lady, and was taken on without any training, nice as she was, she couldn't really help with his work. James had not really learned any decent maths since Year 1, when he was five, so with some initial help from a friend who is a teacher, I have started on a programme that aims to give him a proper working familiarity with numbers. One of the advantages of home educating is that you really can gear things to the specific needs of your child, which in our case are compounded by the fact that James has Pathological Demand Avoidance Syndrome, as well as Asperger's. He will comply only if you approach things in the right way, and I have come up with my own methods of dealing with him, which are far more effective than for him to be just sitting in a classroom doing nothing. There seem to be no set rules on home education, but I had some useful guidelines on my rights from the organisation Education Otherwise.'

Prospective home educators often worry about issues of social integration that can be crucial for ASD children. Those who have taken the plunge tend to be adamant that their children do not miss out socially. Certainly, you can make sure that there are plenty of out-of-school activities, sports and clubs to fill in the social gaps, but it does seem that an element of isolation is built in to this choice, and if you feel that your child needs the regular company of other children to learn essential social skills (even if they might actually be happier in solitary state) then you need to consider this option carefully.

I have helped Jack, an ASD child who was home-educated, over the last few years, and so I can see the advantages and disadvantages of this choice from both sides. I really think it was the best option for him at the time, and it can work out very well with the right tutors.

Jack's mother Kate describes how he came to be home-educated.

'Jack was at a very tough and disciplined school. He was unhappy, and the school really wasn't dealing with the issues that he had. He had a great relationship with some of the teachers but others seemed to feel that he was constantly naughty. There was no mechanism to get the teachers to do things with Jack that we knew would be helpful, however much we suggested them. Jack's lead diagnosis is Asperger's, but in common with a lot of people with this diagnosis, he has dyspraxic tendencies as well, and this is the seat

of his organisational problems. As a parent you know some of the behaviour is infuriating, but you just learn to get into the habit of it, teachers are not necessarily so tolerant or so understanding.

'Try to find a school that will be receptive to your child's needs. With hindsight, I wonder if we had shopped around for a more sympathetic school Jack might not have had to pull out. That said, with Jack we felt that if we moved him to a less academically rigorous school, the problem that he was difficult in lessons where he was bored would be worse and there would be less discipline and more distraction, which he struggled with.

'It is a full-time job running one set of GCSEs when homeschooling. I had to co-ordinate it all. I was effectively running a school with just one pupil. One advantage is that you can be flexible. Jack was tutored four days a week, and on a Friday he and I used to visit museums, exhibitions, anything that would interest him. We even went on cookery courses.

'Jack does think differently from the mainstream, and has particular problems with learning for exams. On the plus side, there are things he grasps extremely fast, and home tutoring meant he could go at his own speed. At school, he'd become very disruptive when bored by having to go over stuff he already understood. This way, he could cover a lot of ground fast. That was useful, because he has other areas where he needs much more input than most students.

'Jack has a typical ASD tendency to interpret exam questions very literally, and often struggles to grasp what the examiner is actually asking for. So his tutors spent extra time with him going over exam techniques and past papers, and helping him find ways to overcome this. One tutor got him to use a highlighter pen to pick out key words in the question (he did this in the actual exam too), to help him focus on the meaning of the question. With an Asperger's child you do have to let them work in their own way – and it will probably be quirky. In physics every time they changed topic Jack would change his accent because it helped him to remember things.

'One major downside of home education is the massive input of time as a parent, even if you are not doing any of the teaching yourself. Jack was there all the time and I didn't get a break from him. At any moment Jack could explode in through the door screaming and shouting. I could be on the phone for work – so there was a constant awareness of his presence. He is so focused – and that is an Asperger's thing – all he could see was that something was stressing him and he needed me to sort it out. There is no point in getting angry with this kind of thing.

'The most obvious disadvantage of home education with any ASD child is that they get fewer opportunities to socialise and interact with other children. In many ways, day-to-day, this can appeal to them, but of course it means they're not learning the things they most need to learn. I did my best to counteract this with lots of friends coming over at weekends, but actually the thing ASD children especially need to learn is how to rub along with people who aren't close friends. So Jack also did things like a weekly drama group, and summer camps and suchlike. Jack would say that he missed the social side and that was hard. Because we live in the country that really was an issue – I don't think it would be so hard if you lived in the middle of town.

'In the end it's a balance. These things didn't give him as good a social training as being at school would have done. However it was better than being at school, which made him frustrated, depressed, stressed and unhappy, not to mention disrupting other students in those lessons where he wasn't motivated. And I have to say that, while he still finds some social situations particularly trying, he comes across as friendly, open and tolerant with other people.

'We found a lovely school for his A levels, and he found it great socially. By that time he was really ready for it and he was so happy to be surrounded by other kids his age. However, despite all that he dropped out of the sixth form at school. He just couldn't cope with having to study things that made no sense to him. He had real trouble organising his time – which is a real ASD danger sign to watch out for. Jack kept saying that he didn't want to fail at something again, and he was doing really well in some subjects, but in the end he said he would be better without doing the A levels, and he has been so happy since then. Now he is doing graphics and wants to go to Art College.'

Kate's tips on how to start home educating

- Decide on your objectives. We wanted Jack to get a good set of academic GCSEs so that he had the option of going back for A levels. In fact Jack got 10 GCSEs – four A*s, four As and two Bs – so we felt that it had all been worthwhile.
- To get through GCSEs you need teachers who can work out the system for you. We found that the kind of teachers who choose to tutor one-to-

one are generally interested in the challenge of a student who is a bit different.

- You have to have some flexibility with tutors – put them on a trial period for your own security, but be aware that this works both ways.
- Clearly this isn't a particularly cheap way to educate a child, and I was lucky to be able to do it. I reckoned it cost about the same as a private school.
- You need to get everything in place as early as possible. You can't leave it until their exam year to sign them up for things.

Matt's journey

School was not easy for Matt, so when he was 14 we took him out for several days a week doing work experience in building with his dad. He still needed routine and it was hard to keep his attention all the time. We learned that if we could keep him busy doing things that he enjoyed he was fine, otherwise he would drift away from what he was supposed to be doing. He enjoyed bricklaying, and we enrolled him on a CITB (Construction Industry Training Board) training course on a block release scheme. He managed to get a moped and got himself to and from the college and completed the course in two years, getting a City and Guilds certificate as a qualified bricklayer. He became much happier and his stress levels went right down. He felt that the pressure was off him and this worked very well for him.

Building helped him bridge a gap into college, where he was happy, but I feel we could have slanted things in a different way if we had known sooner what his interests were. Because ASD children are often developmentally and emotionally behind, they often don't get given the time in their schooldays to focus on or discover what they really want to do or be. But that is true for a lot of teenagers.

Things to consider when you make your choice

Mainstream school

- Will give a chance to integrate more into the everyday world.
- May be the best option for academically able children.

- May require ASD children to conform to rules that baffle them and punish for non-compliance.
- May not have special needs qualified teachers – quite unlikely to have had an opportunity to do any courses on autism.
- Teachers may not understand your child's problems.
- Teachers calling you in for every little thing your child does, making you feel awful and not understanding your problems at all.
- Not all mainstream schools have the capability to address complex needs.
- ASD children are very vulnerable to bullying and can be miserable in the mainstream.

Special school

- Will understand your child and his or her ways.
- More hands-on teaching, more one-to-one.
- Will give the chance to be with others like them – this may not be such a good thing for those with ASD.
- May not push your child enough – there can be a tendency to settle at the lowest common denominator.
- Teachers with specialist skills are more likely to be found in special schools.
- Small groups; work geared to their ability; lots of support – good for confidence.
- Children used to a small group may well become anxious and unable to function properly in a big mainstream class. This often becomes an issue on transfer from primary to secondary.
- ASD children get a feeling of security and routine from a small special school.

Home school

- A child who is really suffering in the mainstream will be able to work better in a home environment, without distraction and the need to conform to puzzling rules.
- They will miss out on social life and you will have to arrange for activities that compensate for this.
- The flexibility of home education is an advantage – you can concentrate on things your child really needs.
- Many ASD children thrive on structure, so you will need to have things very well organised.

- Finding tutors, or doing the teaching yourself, is a fairly substantial undertaking.

The main point is that for some children the stimulus of the mainstream is important, while for others the sheltered environment of a special school or even education at home, may give them the security they need. The choice should be available to all, so that each individual child can benefit from the education that best suits him or her. Sadly, at present, it is often far from straightforward for ASD children and their parents to access this choice.

You have to look at what is best for the individual child. Matt, for instance, would not have coped in a special school. I wanted him to have normal experiences and in consequence we had problems with him trying smoking, skiving off school and all the rest. Clearly, this would not be the right solution for everyone; some children simply couldn't survive the mainstream. People who understand ASD will know that children like Matt are often happier at school than at home, because you don't have rigid timetables at home and you do at school – and of course they find that very reassuring.

Useful contacts

The Advisory Centre for Education (ACE) is an independent charity offering information about state education and telephone advice on subjects such as special educational needs: www.ace-ed.org.uk (helpline: 0300 0115 142).

Parents for Inclusion was set up with the aim of helping disabled children learn, make friends and have a voice in ordinary school. On offer are workshops and courses for parents and professionals, guidance, advocacy and support: www.parentsforinclusion.org.

Education Otherwise is a national support charity for home-educators: www.education-otherwise.org (helpline: 0845 478 6345).

12

Problems at school

Much as we all wish that this was not the case, parents have found that some teachers still reject the diagnosis of ASD. In the light of all the research, all the knowledge, and even the fact that the diagnosis is coming from experts, there is still an undercurrent of thinking that these are just naughty children. A lot of 11-year-olds with ASD are very bright. Teachers can easily be confused by this brightness and responsiveness into thinking that the child should be able to do things that they simply cannot do. In the current climate where inclusion when possible is the stated aim, schools have to move with the times and provide appropriate help for everybody, but for some children who become embattled in the system, home education may end up being the answer.

In meetings with Matt's school I sometimes found it really hard not to yell out 'But that is your job, to accommodate each child's needs.' The point is that there is a knack to teaching autistic children. You do have to deal with them in a different way to the rest of the class and I know it is hard. I made mistakes myself and I was living with the problem every day, so I know it is hard for outsiders. Schools should try to understand what a struggle it can be for parents of special-needs children, and be more sympathetic. A recent report said that nearly half of parents in the category experienced problems with the educational system, and I can well believe it.

So, given that the system imposes strains both on parent and teacher – not to mention the pupil – what can you do as a parent to make things easier for everyone? One thing is to promote awareness of what your child's condition, in our case Asperger syndrome, will mean for the teacher.

It helps if the teacher is aware of the following.

- ASD children will find it really hard to learn the social skills they need for school, and may not have many reserves left for classwork – at least initially. Such children may also find it hard to understand the need to fit in and obey the rules.
- A teacher needs to be very explicit in giving instructions and to check that the child has really understood them and knows what they are meant to do. The teacher should start instructions with the child's name or they may not realise that they are the one being talked to.
- It will help if the teacher bears in mind that this child may not understand visual clues from facial expression or behaviour, or have much idea of the effect of his behaviour on other children.
- A child with ASD will prefer familiar things and may resist moving from what they know.
- The teacher may feel that the point of a lesson is obvious, but the ASD child may focus on something quite different.

These are just a few of the basic issues that the teacher is going to have to take on board when your child enters the class. There are guidelines available, but it will help everyone if you bear in mind that the teacher has to make a lot of effort to incorporate your child's needs into what may well be a full and lively class, and be understanding in your approach as a parent.

I think more practical training and understanding of how ASD children function would be a huge help and I don't think that there is enough of it anywhere. I think the learning support assistants (LSAs – in class to give one-to-one support for each child with special needs) who work with these children need to be chosen very carefully, and properly trained so that they understand the ASD child's condition and needs. An LSA is a crucial element in mainstream education for boys like Matt, but LSA training for special needs, which is not compulsory anyway, does not go into certain conditions, including ASD. So the people directly involved in their day-to-day school life may not have any specific training. Even one week's specific training would make everybody's life so much easier.

If you get the chance to talk things through with your LSA, you can make sure that they understand what they will be dealing with.

The LSA needs to know how to:

- interpret situations for the child and show them what they need to do, using simple language and one instruction at a time and always going at the child's pace
- help them learn social skills such as turn-taking, while guiding other children in the class in how to interact with them
- understand an ASD child's problems with language and communication and make things clear to them when they are confused
- anticipate and try to avoid things that will cause anxiety
- appreciate that the approach for an ASD child is different to other special needs. They may be happy with the routine and structure of fairly solitary learning and uncomfortable with playing with classmates.

School life by Matthew Keith Brealy, 14

'When I wake up I find it hard because my body feels like staying in bed. Once I do get up and have to put my clothes on, sometimes I forget to put my boxers on and just put my trousers on. When I have to pack my bag I need to remember to pack my PE kit because all the time I forget. Sometimes I have not remembered to clean my teeth and little things like that. When I get to school I go to my first lesson. The teacher doesn't give me enough time to get my stuff ready. When they ask a question they don't give me enough time to answer them. Your brain needs to think so then they asked someone else and I get a low mark and I get funny spells if I get them when a teacher is speaking to me I have to make them say it again and they get annoyed with me. If a teacher shouts at me I laugh because I find it funny. I prefer if they talk to me and not shout at me. I don't like it when a teacher has shouted at me because I did something wrong and I don't realise what I've done.'

How to make school less stressful

Sad to say, parents in mainstream school can probably expect hostility from other parents who feel that ASD children are just disruptive and hog the teacher's time and attention. This is something that you need to be prepared for. I feel there should be more liaison with other parents and teachers for ASD parents, maybe mediation from someone like myself who understands both sides of the situation at first hand. If the school is not being helpful or understanding, what can you do?

How can you sort out continuing problems with a particular teacher?

- You need to keep in touch with your child's work and progress so you know and understand what the teacher is saying.
- If the teacher is hard to talk to, go to the special needs teacher and explain your worries. He or she should be able to help you.
- You should take on board what the teacher has to say, as you need to be able to see the situation from both sides.
- If you are still unhappy with the results, you need to see the head and ask for an action plan to be made to help all concerned.
- You can go to the educational psychologist for the school area who will help put an individual education plan together which can help everyone who is concerned with the child.
- If all else fails, you can ask that your child is not taught by this teacher but it is best if you can meet half way.
- Teachers don't always realise that they have to explain things over and over again to ASD children, so if you can – tactfully – remind them of the parameters of the condition; it will help.

Trouble in class by Matthew Keith Brealy, 14

'I've lost count of how many times I've been in trouble because the teacher has told me to copy a question from the board. I do it, because that's what I've been asked to do, but then I get in trouble for not putting the answer down too. But he didn't ask me to do that.'

It didn't matter how often this happened, Matt still wouldn't realise – so the teacher should. Children like Matt will only do what they are asked. He would get put outside the classroom door for not concentrating. When the teacher asked Matt if he would come back in and concentrate he would say 'no', because he knew he couldn't concentrate, and then his reply got him into even more trouble.

Of course, Matt was not an entirely innocent victim in all this. People might have thought that Matt's attitude was confrontational because if an LSA said that he needed to do something he would always say 'why?'

I am sure that was really irritating, but, unfortunately, he really did want to know why.

Matt was always losing his pencil case and other stuff and getting punished. He would take it out of his bag to put something in and then forget to put it back. Then he would be frustrated and surprised because he knew he started the day off with it and was baffled by its disappearance. The problems he had in school, I'm afraid, are fairly typical. It is a widespread problem. The National Autistic Society says that over 10% of queries it receives each year are education-related.

I started training in special needs when my daughter started school and I saw a girl there who was just like Matt. I helped out with her and then did an NVQ. I found that I really enjoyed the studying and had learned so much from Matt, which I took into my special needs teaching. What pushed me into it was that Matt was having so many problems at school and I wondered how many other parents were having the same problems.

Matt was best with hands-on subjects at school. He had the concentration of a gnat, was easily distracted and had little memory, then he would get into trouble because he couldn't remember. I would have liked him to repeat a year but the special needs teacher felt that it was important for Matt to be quite cool and in with his mates and it would be humiliating for him to be kept down with younger ones. School was more important socially and for the acquisition of life skills than academically for him. It was not worth him pushing for exams and we knew that we would look in the direction of practical jobs when he finished.

There are still a handful of parents who don't want their children to play with anyone not 'normal' and so the cycle of prejudice continues. I think it is good that they have to be more inclusive in schools. I think it may make other parents confront their prejudices a bit.

Those difficult times of day

Assembly

Assembly has all the ingredients an ASD child will hate: noisy groups going into and out of the hall, the necessity to sit quietly, in closely packed rows, where they may be stuck in the middle rather than at the edges which they would prefer, and then the need to sit quiet and still while someone goes on and on about something boring. There are lots of rules here that are different to the classroom and may be hard to grasp. If you think your child is going to have trouble with all this when they start school, there are a few things you could try.

- Ask if your child has to go into assembly right from the start, especially if you think it will make them anxious. Maybe they could spend some quiet time with a one-to-one activity before the hustle of the day in class.
- If they can gradually start coming into assembly at their own pace, success may be more likely.
- Make sure your child understands the rules and what they have to do, and see if there is another child who can help them out and keep an eye on them and be their 'buddy'. If they have a one-to-one helper, they should sit with them.
- Ask if your child can sit at the edge so that they will feel more comfortable.
- Explain how long assembly will last – use egg timers to help with the idea of the time.

Break time

Break time is quite often hard for ASD children as it is not structured. When they are uncertain what to do they may act inappropriately or isolate themselves from other children, so you may need to ask someone to organise their play.

Here are some things you can try to help with break times.

- Encourage them to join a break-time club.
- Ask to see if they can sit in the library.
- See if the school uses the 'buddy' system, which is where another child is your child's special companion and helps them play or sits and reads with them.
- If your child likes to be alone, then find out if there is a suitable place for them.
- See if the school has a time-out room (where children can go to be on their own and undisturbed).
- If they want to join in with the others, but don't know how, try to teach them some ways to start up conversations without people thinking they are weird.

Lunch time

Lunch is a noisy and sociable time that can be a nightmare for ASD children, who will need strategies to help them to cope.

- If they find queuing difficult, see if the teachers will let them be at the front or back of the queue, rather than anywhere in the middle, which may make them very anxious.
- Make sure the dinner ladies know what has been arranged for them.
- Try to teach them a few simple bits of conversation to help them to join in with the children at their table.

Working with classmates

Joining in with others can be very problematic for your ASD child, who may not have much awareness of the feelings of other people or of the effect his or her behaviour can have on them. Some ASD children will be tense and anxious if someone is even sitting too near them. Working in groups is the norm for a lot of lessons these days, so you will need some strategies to help your child get used to working with others.

- You know how much social contact your child can cope with before anxiety sets in: make sure the teacher knows too.
- Ask if your child can sit at the edge of group activity to start with, perhaps on the other side of the support assistant.
- The support assistant can encourage your child to try turn-taking tasks, at first with him or her and then in a supervised way with another child, then, if all goes well, just with the other child.
- Tell the teacher of any special skills or interests your child has which he or she may be able to draw on in class.
- If your child can cope with it, invite a classmate to your house for tea. It can be very helpful if you encourage this before your child starts at the school.

Staying in school

Matt had a bad habit of wandering off site during the day. If he wanted to buy a drink or something, he would just go to the shop, quite forgetting that he was supposed to stay in the school grounds. In the end I put a laminated note in his bag where his money was which read 'Matt don't leave the school premises' and that seemed to do the trick.

School holidays

Most ASD children find the disruption to routine of the school holidays rather a hard thing to cope with. Matt used to be awful, but later he loved the holidays best. I found that starting up a timetable at home sorted out the problem.

- Timetable each day of the holidays.
- Work out what you are going to do and keep it structured.
- Get your child to help with the timetable.
- Let them help choose activities.
- Have a time out zone in the house in case things get too much. If there is one at school your child will probably want one at home, too.

Bullying

This is a worry for all parents, and children with any disability can be especially vulnerable to bullying. I was lucky as Matt's older brother was at the same school and he took good care of him, but you still get the odd day where other children do say things that upset your child.

On the other hand, children with ASD can say the most awful things to other children, and I have used this fact to explain to Matt how people feel when he says mean things to them. With other ASD children I have worked on making up a 'feelings folder' with different pictures showing feelings like sad/happy/cross; then asking them how they are feeling themselves and how they think what they have said has made someone else feel. The child will point to the picture and you can explain the feeling to them as best you can. As we know, ASD children tend to have real problems with relating to others socially; misunderstanding and lack of eye contact mean that they have immense difficulty interpreting much communication. See p118 for more on cyberbullying.

How to help combat bullying

- 'Buddy' them with someone at school – an older child or more mature classmate.
- Help them understand bullying – from both sides. Reading leaflets about bullying will be useful here.

- Listen to your child and watch out for unaccountable changes in behaviour, so you can see the special needs teacher as soon as any bullying starts.
- Keep a diary on your child – a pattern behind the bullying might emerge.
- For a child without speech you need an illustrated 'feelings folder' so they can show you what is wrong.
- Think of your child's feelings but also think that your child might be the one who is provoking the bullying by saying unkind things.

Cyberbullying – or not

When it comes to something like cyberbullying Matt would say 'Just don't look at it' and for a lot of ASD children it really is that simple. If a child is being upset, you can teach them to block people who upset them from, for example, their Facebook account.

It may be that an ASD child is accused of cyberbullying and this can be more of an issue of misunderstanding. They can make hurtful remarks to others without realising, and we have to make them understand that they should not.

In general, ASD children are probably less vulnerable to online bullying than other children and it's verbal bullying that can be more of a problem. But as autistic children tend to take things very literally they may find things more offensive than they are intended to be. If an autistic child takes something the wrong way, it may be a skewed ASD perception and an inappropriate use of the buzzword of bullying. That said, ASD children do stick out as different and can be the subject of bullying. If you are worried, write a letter to the teacher and ask for a copy of the school's anti-bullying policy.

Useful contacts

Advisory Centre for Education (ACE) offers telephone advice on bullying: www.ace-ed.org.uk (helpline: 0300 0115 142).

On the issue of cyberbullying of children with autism/Asperger's you can find helpful advice at www.autism.org.uk.

Ways to make school life run more smoothly

Allow plenty of time to get ready in the morning. If the child is rushed to start with, they will be anxious all day and will not concentrate.

- Make sure the child has packed up everything they need for that day.
- If you have other children, enlist their help as much as possible so that you can concentrate on helping your ASD child to get ready.
- Make sure you drop off at the same time and place each day.
- Picking them up at the same time, same place each afternoon also helps routine.
- Have a drink and a snack ready when you pick them up after school to help them unwind.
- Give them the space and quiet time they need to unwind after school.
- Give the teacher written information to help get to know your child. I prepared a detailed folder on Matt, his ways and how we dealt with him at home.
- If something has happened which has made the child anxious – a favourite toy has gone missing, their shirt is the Wrong One, or any one of countless other daily catastrophes – you need to tell the teacher first thing or they cannot make allowances for any change in behaviour and this will upset everyone.

One thing that really helped Jack when he was being educated at home, and which I think could be really useful in schools, was what we called 'gripe sessions'. We had two or three a week to start with, during which he could offload anything that was bothering him. We had a little book where he could write any problems he had during the week that he wanted me to try to iron out for him. Whether it was something at home that he didn't want to go to his mum with, something with the tutor, something with homework or any projects where he knew that he just couldn't reach the target and it was getting to him. He could offload everything and it really helped him.

Jack was so different afterwards. He was much more relaxed – he had got everything that had built up in the week off his chest. I would address all his issues in a way he could understand – where perhaps he had misunderstood something I could put it in perspective for him and then the problem went away.

After a while I felt I had made myself redundant from that part of the job. Once you can teach a child how to cope with a problem, or how to express it to someone at home so that they can sort it out, then you don't get the same build-up of anxiety. If they know there is a structure for ironing out their problems then things don't turn into mountains. You just have to watch out that, with a regular fixed time, they don't start thinking up complaints to fill the slot when nothing is really wrong.

These children do have a tendency to hold on to problems and store them up – they can't find a way to deal with things themselves – so you have to do it for them or, at best, say you have worked out a plan that you can try together to deal with the problem. It is very good for them to start to feel that they have some power to deal with problems for themselves.

13

Know your rights

The education, health and care plan

Any special provision for your child, such as special schooling, a learning support assistant in a mainstream class, speech therapy and much more besides are all accessed by means of the education, health and care plan (in England; the statement of special educational needs in other parts of the UK) so if your child has been diagnosed with ASD then it is in all your interests to get into the system.

The Children and Families Act 2014 incorporates changes to the special educational needs (SEN) support system. In England the new education, health and care (EHC) plan covers educational, health and social care needs for each individual child with special needs from birth to age 25 (if still in education) under one umbrella. This has replaced the old statement of special educational needs (SSEN). The idea is that these more across-the-board plans replace education-only statements and support a child's broader range of needs, for example, encompassing education and social care. Assessments are still carried out under the auspices of your local authority. If your child has an existing statement, that will be transferred to an EHC plan over the next few years. Arrangements are different in other parts of the UK, and you can find helpful information and guidance at www.autism.org.uk.

Just as getting a statement was the passport to all the help and support we eventually managed to access for Matt, the new plan will be crucial for your child, and it is worth jumping through all the hoops to get it.

Help with the bureaucracy

I have two bulging files at home full of the correspondence it took to get Matt statemented. I really wanted to have his needs acknowledged and helped – and in order to do that I had to have a statement of special educational needs. There were times during the lengthy and tortuous process when I felt as if everyone was against me. It seems that not much has changed in this area, and I really wonder why it has to be so hard and why you always feel as if you are in combat with the system.

IASS (Information, Advice and Support Services) are free services to be found in every local authority, where you can get advice on how to fight your way through the official jargon, and which steps you have to follow to get your child an EHC assessment and plan. Someone from the organisation will help you to fill out the forms you need and give you support in preparing for and attending meetings. Find details of your local service at www.iassnetwork.org.uk.

The letter about Matt was one of the hardest things I have ever had to do and it still haunts me. You have to write about your child from birth up to date. Putting everything we had been through down in black and white and having to write down all the things that my son could not do, for someone else to read, was incredibly difficult. It seemed so condemning to be writing such a letter – the exact opposite of how you want to be as a mother. My protective side came out and I wanted to say 'But it's ok, I love him' as I couldn't bear other people to think badly of my child.

Tips for parents

- Consult the Special Educational Needs and Disability (SEND) Code of Practice at the Department for Education (DfE): www.gov.uk. Although long and complex, this is a surprisingly straightforward read and it is important to note that the SEND system has been comprehensively re-structured and now covers ages 0 to 25 in one system.
- Ask to see local authority guidance/policy for special educational needs.
- Keep copies of all letters and take notes in meetings.
- Keep a diary of your child's progress and the difficulties you encounter.
- Don't be afraid to speak out.
- Always ask if you don't know something or don't understand – organisations such as IASS are there to help.

- Find out your rights in the school. You are allowed to see the special needs policies of the school.
- Read the policies thoroughly and take notes if you need to.
- Don't think you are being a pain. You want what is right for your child.

Useful contacts

IPSEA (Independent Parental Special Education Advice) – an organisation defending children's right to special education provision, with a very informative website: www.ipsea.org.uk.

Information, Advice and Support Services (IASS) Network – supports parents and carers of children with special educational needs. Contact through www.iassnetwork.org.uk.

Mencap – www.mencap.org.uk.

Benefits and how to get them

The complicated away of benefits available and the range of eligibility for them can deter people from even applying, but you may well be entitled to more than you think, and it is only sensible to claim anything you are entitled to.

Disability Living Allowance is available for people who need help with personal care and/or getting around. Find out more at www.gov.uk/help-for-disabled-child.

A guide to claiming DLA for children with brain disorders including ASD is available from www.cerebra.org.uk.

www.disabilityrightsuk.org has information and services developed by and for disabled people and includes fact sheets on benefits and how to apply for them.

The struggle to get help close to home

Just as ASD varies widely, so does the availability of care and resources – and some places are very much at a disadvantage. For instance, it is only thanks to years of campaigning by his determined father that a severely autistic boy with a distressing history of self-harm is going to be able to move back to his home county, Cornwall, from the nearest facility which has been able to help him – in Birmingham.

Josh's father Stephen tells his story – which starts in a way that many ASD parents will recognise.

'Josh seemed like a normal baby at first but between the ages of two and three it became clear that he wasn't responding or speaking. Hearing tests were ok so we had to look further, and by the time he was three he was diagnosed as severely autistic. The early diagnosis really helped. Josh has a high capacity of understanding and learning but low attention span. He does not speak normally but has his own words for things so he is communicative – but this can be via screaming or hitting himself. He can ask for things using his own "words" and the people who care for him know what these words mean.

'Three years ago, age 11, he started self-harming very badly and screaming through the night, disturbing his siblings. His injuries became life-threatening, and no one could find out why he was so distressed. He has lost most of his bottom lip and half his tongue. He was sent to an assessment unit in Birmingham, which was meant to be a short-term thing, but he has now been there for 26 months, far from the family.

'Our campaign to find something nearer to our home in Cornwall has led to meetings with government ministers. People have listened, with the result that private providers in Cornwall will set up what he needs. Josh wanted to come home to Cornwall and feel that he is near his family. It will be much easier for everyone to visit him regularly now, and will help lots of other children.

'As a parent I would say that you have to know when you can't deal with it yourself any more, no matter how much you want to. We made the decision to call in help when we felt that we couldn't deal with the situation that Josh's problems had become life-threatening. Finding the right help was really not easy and we have felt embattled at a local level. In the end the care plan was that we would travel to Birmingham to see him. They have made as much progress as they can to keep him safe there and I have clocked up some 43,000 miles on the train over these years. His family attachments are still strong despite the long period of separation and the best thing for Josh now, mentally, physically and emotionally is to be back in his home county, near us all, and able to have a run on the beach from time to time.'

14

Treatments and therapies

There are lots of therapies and treatments around, some costly, some completely free. You never know what may work for your child: 'Don't knock it until you have tried it' is my motto. Some things have worked for us, some have worked for other people, so what is included below can be seen as a collection of suggestions. Although we found that Melatonin helped Matt to sleep when he was younger (see p83) we did not choose to go down the medication route with him, so this is not included here.

Massage

A daily massage dramatically cut down on the incidence of tantrums for Alexander Lubbock, who is autistic, and his father was delighted that the treatment made such a difference.

'A friend in our village who was aware of Alexander's constant anxiety offered to try to massage him every day for six months as an experiment, and it led to an absolutely massive transformation. It was brilliant for Alexander; we went from about six tantrums a day to one a month. Initially we had sessions of 30 to 45 minutes a day, which went down to three times a week, still with the same good effects. At first she came to the house and she had to follow him around and just rub his shoulders while he was at his computer and so on; pretty soon he was co-operating and then he would go her house and just hop on the massage table. It seems so logical that massage should be beneficial,

I can't believe we never thought of it before. These children are always so tense and anxious and they have no reserves to deal with problems when they arise.'

Cranial osteopathy

Lesley Burton found that cranial osteopathy worked wonders for her son Eddie.

'About four to five weeks after a session he just gets to the point where he is doing handstands all the time or bouncing everywhere and we realise it is time to go back to the osteopath and that demonstrably sorts him out a bit. We first tried it when he was about 18 months old and he didn't really like it, but there were noticeable benefits.

'I take him to the Osteopathic Centre for Children. Eddie was very difficult at first, he didn't like hands on his head or on his back and just wanted to leave, but we go regularly now and it is the making of him. You need to stick with these things if they are not too traumatic for them. With Eddie certainly there was a turning point when he suddenly seemed to realise that he always felt better after he had let them do the massage and now he will run in and let them get on with it.

'The Osteopathic Centre for Children is a charity where you pay what you can afford. They say that autistic children have got a very tight head and with Eddie they say that the part of his brain that should deal with speech and language – the frontal lobe – is very tight and very restricted, which is typical of autistic children who are non-verbal. The treatment is so gentle and non-invasive, it has been a real success for us.'

The Osteopathic Centre for Children: www.occ.uk.com (020 8875 5290).

Acupuncture

Long before her son Toby's diagnosis with Asperger's, Maddie Templar discovered how beneficial acupuncture could be for him.

'My acupuncturist suggested we try treating Toby when he was small, after I told her about his persistent cough and his behavioural problems. We found straight away that there were distinct benefits.

'It is fairly stressful being Toby, and he can't seem to get rid of the stress for himself, it just builds and builds until he has a tantrum: acupuncture really helps him. What seems to happen is that Toby's behaviour gets worse the day after his acupuncture, then somehow it clears and he can be relaxed for weeks until it is time to go for another session.

'He is very calm about the actual treatment, which is done while he watches television. For children up to about the age of ten the acupuncturist uses an electrical machine that passes a tiny current over the acupuncture points, so there are no needles for him to worry about.'

Find an acupuncturist through the British Acupuncture Council: www.acupuncture.org.uk (020 8735 0400).

Speech therapy

Speech therapy is invaluable for ASD children, but is not always easily available. The national shortage of speech therapists is highlighted by Lady Astor of Hever, whose autistic daughter, Olivia, found speech therapy particularly effective.

'We couldn't get speech therapy through our LEA [Local Education Authority], so I paid for a speech and language therapist for years. Olivia had weekly lessons, which were wonderful, and I learned a lot myself about how speech and language develop.

'Speech therapy and occupational therapy should be accessible to everyone, but there is a terrible shortage of therapists. It takes them so long to qualify and if they are paid on NHS rates they don't make any money at all so they all go private. If the government doesn't give them a living salary, it is very difficult to get them to go and teach in schools. These services should be available for children who have any kind of special needs. They are the fundamentals – the building blocks – and they should be within education.'

Nutritional therapy

A lot of ASD children have food phobias and some parents find it really helpful to get advice from a nutritionist. I have already talked about the problems I had getting Matt to eat anything new when he was younger.

He is pretty good now, but I know that, for a lot of people with ASD, food remains a problem. The wilder reaches of the condition can be the home of eating habits that are, to say the least, erratic.

Parents who have battled with the nothing-yellow-ever diet, the exactly-the-same-thing-every-single-day-for-always diet, the only-white-food diet, the just-six-Smarties-and-nothing-else diet, and many more besides, will know how hard it is to ensure that basic nutrients get into the system, as nutritional therapist Sally Child is well aware. She recommends a full nutritional assessment if you have concerns, so that any testing, dietary changes and supplementation can be discussed and tailored to the individual child. Sally explains:

'There are several underlying factors which can affect the symptoms of an autistic child. I would investigate these and test accordingly. As they often eat very few foods and allergy/toxicity is common, increasing the range is important but difficult.

'It is virtually impossible to get them out of quirky fads as this is part of the condition and provides security, but it is possible to reduce them by balancing blood sugar levels. Asperger sufferers often only eat alone and at night, for instance. Protein is often low and fruit and veg non-existent. Some remedies will be recommended as a result of test results. I would say that the older the child the less responsive they are to dietary intervention, but there is always something we can do to improve their nutritional status.'

Find a dietitian via your GP or the British Dietetic Association: www.bda. uk.com.

Music therapy

Music therapy is increasingly used as part of early intervention programmes for ASD children. It has been found that music can stimulate communication for them, and music therapy is based on the idea that our innate responsiveness to music transcends disability. Sessions will be either one-to-one or in a group and, as consistency is important for ASD children, will be held in the same place each week, in a quiet room with no distractions. Music therapy is not the same as music lessons – the child is not learning to play an instrument though they may acquire some musical skills during the sessions. The therapist uses percussion, tuned instruments or her own voice to respond in creative ways to sounds produced by the child to make a musical 'language'.

Find a therapist in your area from the British Association for Music Therapy: www.bamt.org or www.nordoff-robbins.org.uk.

Sensory integration therapy

This method aims to help people whose senses are over-sensitive by flooding them with sensory experiences such as swinging, rolling, jumping and spinning. It is provided by specially trained occupational therapists. Further information from www.sensoryintegration.org.uk.

Auditory integration training

This is a complex method which some people find very effective. It aims to help those with auditory processing difficulties by desensitising children to the sounds that bother them, leaving them more responsive to sounds in general, including speech. The treatment involves a number of sessions listening to music modified to avoid the individual hypersensitivities.

Research Autism

More details about these therapies can be found at www. researchautism.net. This is a good starting point for parents looking for impartial advice on some of the therapies available. It may help prevent you wasting time on therapies that will be pointless in your case and direct you towards some good ones.

Relaxation

I have heard of people who have had very positive results with relaxation classes – if you find one in your area, you could go with your child! If not, it might be worth investing in a relaxation CD and listening to it with your child. In fact, if your child likes to sit and listen, it might be worth considering meditation: I have heard of this producing surprisingly good results.

Hypnotherapy

Jack has had hypnotherapy for specific problems. For example, we discovered that he simply couldn't concentrate during exams because every time anyone coughed, or dropped a pencil, or an invigilator walked down the aisles, he lost all focus. He came out of his very first such exam – in a subject he was strong in – in tears because he'd been unable to get to the end of the paper. Hypnotherapy was brilliant, enabling Jack to imagine himself inside a bubble in which nothing outside it disturbed him in any way, though he was still aware of the invigilator telling them it was time to stop, and anything else essential.

Pets as therapy

A lot of new research shows that pets, especially dogs, can be wonderful for ASD children, helping them learn about loving relationships, and sometimes helping them to feel successful in a relationship for the first time.

> ### Pets by Matt Brealy, 24
> *'It made me relaxed and happy to be around our dog and cat. When you are young and autistic you find animals easier to get along with than people. The emotions are easy to understand. Having the cat on my lap made me feel relaxed. I respect animals. You can appreciate how amazing they are.'*

Animals can be wonderful with ASD children, but there are a few tips that may help.

- Watch the animal and always take care. Often Labradors or retrievers are specially trained, but an ASD child is unpredictable and you should never leave them alone with a pet unless you are very sure that they would never harm or provoke the animal and unless you know the animal is completely reliable.
- If you don't have a family pet you could take your child to a petting zoo, or city farm, to get them used to animals and to lose any fear they may have. It could be the start of a real enthusiasm for them.

Surfing

Some of the activities found to be beneficial may surprise you. The mother of a severely autistic boy in Devon reports that he has had a fantastic time with a local surf school that runs lessons for autistic children. 'On the beach and in the sea, these children, who have challenging behaviours and a limited understanding of dangers, can have a rare and special few moments of freedom.'

Some parents will want to leave the treatments alone, but, as Charlotte Moore, the mother of two autistic boys, wrote in her fascinating book about them, *George and Sam*, 'Powerlessness is bad for parents. If trying a diet or behaviour-modification programme makes them feel that their frustrated love for their child is being put to good use, then that's a good thing. I've tried a lot of treatments and have gained something from most of them.'

15

Getting help from health professionals

Dealing with the doctors

Your GP will be your first port of call with any concerns though, as we mentioned in Chapter 1, it may be that you speak to your health visitor first if your child is very young. Ideally, your GP will then refer you on to a consultant – possibly a specialist paediatrician, a psychologist or educational psychologist who should have expertise in ASD.

GPs

Doctors can help a lot if you have a child with an ASD, but I feel that if they understood what we go through each day then they could help much better. Many know the medical condition but not what it actually means to families like us. But if you are lucky enough to have a good GP who actually listens to you then half the battle is won. Do go to the GP and explain.

- See a doctor you know will listen even if it is not your usual doctor.
- Go back again if you are not happy with the outcome.
- Take in any observations you have done on your child's behaviour and habits if you think they might be relevant.

Consultants

You see the consultant a lot more than the GP, I found, and my consultant for Matt was fantastic and listened to all I had to say. I took the video of Matt's night terrors to him and he prescribed Melatonin. I was so relieved when it helped Matt out of the worst of his sleeping problems. You can also get help from them for school as they write letters and explain your child's problems.

- Don't be afraid of the consultants as they are there to help you.
- Tell them everything as even small details could help.
- Let them see a film of your child in action if you cannot explain behaviour.
- Show them any written observations of your child you have made.
- If you are not happy with your consultant ask to see someone else.

Roles of the health professionals who might be involved with your ASD child

- GP – your first port of call for health services, will refer you on to specialists.
- Health visitor – specialist nurse with further training in child development, family health and welfare, will visit at home.
- Community paediatrician – doctor who is an expert in the health and development of children, especially those with disorders including ASD. Often diagnose ASD conditions and know when to refer child on to other specialists.
- Paediatrician – organises hospital services for sick children.
- School nurse – has expertise in conditions that may affect children's ability to learn; provides a link between school and health services.
- Educational psychologist – specialist who has studied how children learn and behave.
- Dietician – provides advice, information and teaching on nutrition and diets.
- Portage worker – uses a home teaching method originating in Portage, Wisconsin; has expertise in working with parents of pre-school children, helping them with developmental difficulties. Get information on the service from your health visitor.

- Speech therapist – can help promote the development of language and communication in people with developmental disabilities.
- Occupational therapist (OT) – expert in understanding how ASD can affect day-to-day activities, gives practical advice to parents on how to reduce everyday problems faced by those with ASDs.

Useful-to-know abbreviations

This is a world awash with jargon. If you can't tell your PSAT from your SENCO, you need to get to know your abbreviations ASAP.

SEN – Special Educational Needs
SENCO – Special Educational Needs Co-ordinator
EP – Educational Psychologist
LST – Learning Support Team
AEO – Area Education Officer
IEP – Individual Education Plan – Teaching plan for children with special educational needs will set targets for your child to achieve within a given time and is regularly reviewed by the school EWO – Education Welfare Officer
PSAT – Pre-School Advisory Teacher
BST – Behaviour Support Team
LEA – Local Education Authority
C of P – Code of Practice
VO – Voluntary Organisation
SpLD – Specific Learning Difficulties
MLD – Moderate Learning Difficulties
EBD – Emotional and Behavioural Difficulties
SLD – Severe Learning Difficulties
PMLD – Profound and Multiple Learning Difficulties

Useful organisations

National Autistic Society: www.autism.org.uk (helpline: 0808 800 4104).

TEACCH: This programme aims to equip people with ASD to live and work more effectively at home and school, in the community and workplace. Various techniques and methods are used as part of individual plans specifically targeted at those with ASD and their families. The aim is to help them improve learning, social and language skills. TEACCH was developed in the USA. For details of the programme in the UK, visit www.autismuk. com.

Contact a Family: a national charity which supports families who have children with different disabilities and special needs. The organisation links with over 500 support and self-help groups, offering support and advice. Parents can be put in touch with a support group or another family whose child has a similar disability: www.cafamily.org.uk (0808 808 3555).

Things are improving

Lesley, mother of Eddie, stresses that in the last ten years many more places to find help and information have appeared:

'A lot of resources and facilities are much better now, though it is still a postcode lottery as to whether you can access them. The Autism Show, the national event for autism takes place each year at ExCeL in London, and in Birmingham and Manchester. It has only started in the last few years but is very well-attended and attracts lots of eminent speakers and offers things like behaviour clinics where the chance to talk to professionals is very welcome. There is a lot more out there than there was ten years ago.'

16

Teenage life – leaving school and thinking about the future

Matt now seems like a completely different person to the boy we wrote about ten years ago. Bright, lively and with a ready smile and masses of eye contact, he is a charming and confident young man, who shows little resemblance to the detached, rather hesitant boy he was when we wrote the original book. All the work we did as a family to help him socially has really paid off.

> **Tips for a 16-year-old by Matt Brealy, 24**
> *'Do what you want to do – don't listen to other people or be led by them. Trust yourself a bit more – give things a go. If you fail you can always get back up and then try and do it again. I was lucky, I had a lot of support from my family, and I know not everyone gets that.'*

The teenage years are a bad enough time for all parents. ASD just adds a shedload more complications. All I can do is tell you how we coped and hope it helps you.

Teenage life

It is bad enough for normal teenagers, with all those hormones flying around. Add those into the ASD mix and you can just imagine the problems and confusion that may ensue.

Here are some tips that I found useful with Matt.

- Let them know you are there to listen to them when they need you.
- Give them space to be teenagers – try to remember what it was like.
- Respect how they are feeling.
- Read them information on feelings they might be getting if they (or you) are not too embarrassed. If this is too awkward, try to get an older sibling or family friend to take on the task.

Matt's early teenage life was, to say the least, eventful. He was invariably very easily led by others, which meant that some of his 'friends' egged him on and he got into all sorts of scrapes, for which he had to be grounded from time to time.

This is one of the areas where you can really see how much Matt has changed. He makes very good decisions about people now, whereas he used to get a little led astray by some of his 'friends'. He is able to see when a person is good or not. It is amazing how he does this: he sees things we don't in people.

> ## Other people by Matt Brealy, 24
> *'I find that I'm very good at judging character. Within the first ten minutes I'll know if I am going to like you or not. I find I can tell by the way someone speaks and their general persona. At the age I am now I know my personality well, so I know if we would clash.'*

- Now may be the time when you have to rethink some of the discipline you use. Do remember to reward good behaviour – ASD teenagers still need as much reinforcement as they did when they were younger.
- They may have a thirst for the new, but they still need the same reassurances and routines they have always had.

> ## Trying new things and feeling safe by Matthew Keith Brealy, 14
>
> *'I like to try everything as if you don't try it how do you know if you like it. I like to know what is going on all the time and when and how so I know what is coming next.'*

Going out

As a teenager Matt loved to go out with his brothers, which taught him a lot about socialising.

- It is really important that ASD teenagers get good examples and practical experience of how to socialise, if that is what they want to do.
- Get a sibling or friend to take them out socially so that they can see how to behave.
- Encourage them to join a youth club, sports club or some other after-school activity.
- You will probably take them out, too, but it is very important for them to get a taste of independent life without you if at all possible. If there are no siblings or dependable friends around, you could get a carer to take them out to the cinema, to a cafe and other places where they can see other people socialising.
- Some teenagers can get a lot out of half-term and holiday courses run locally – 'rock school', dancing, anything that interests them.

Zena Fisher runs holiday play schemes for youngsters with additional needs up to age 18. She finds that having different levels of need together works well, and can be beneficial on both sides, giving a rare opportunity for profoundly disabled teenagers to mix with the more able. The more able ones get a sense of responsibility that is not often available to them in a more mainstream setting. While there is a real and serious lack of provision for over-18s, a lot of Zena's former service users come back to the schemes as helpers, and they love the feeling of going to work, and of earning some pocket money and wearing the same T-shirts as the staff. Look out for such voluntary schemes locally, as they can give a real sense of self-worth to youngsters who may struggle to find any form of employment.

Help for teenagers

The lack of provision in some parts of the country is highlighted in the case of 20-year-old Eva. Her mother, Eloise, explains her predicament.

'We are among the first in the county to try to do the new education, health and care plan. This would give us a budget for suitable education, training or work placement – but there isn't anything right for Eva here. It is a brick wall – we can't request anything, as there is nothing here.

'Eva had a lot of trouble getting a diagnosis in her teens. Like a lot of girls she had managed to hide her differences for a long time, and did well at mainstream school until in her teenage years she became more and more aware that she was different from everyone else; that there were social aspects of life that she simply couldn't deal with. She has sensory processing disorder and things just got harder and harder for her.

'Eva really wants to be able to work. She loves horses so she is doing Parelli training (where you adapt to the horse rather than the other way round) and working with horses, and I am fighting for this to be funded by the LEA [Local Education Authority].

'Usefully, we have found a wonderful community group where professionals work with special needs and volunteers, and they do fantastic work in the visual arts, dance and movement. It is a question of exploring as many avenues as possible as we struggle to find ways back into education.'

Romance

Matt came late to romance, I think because he was a few years behind in some of his development. We worried about him being taken for a ride as he is very soft-hearted and would never see if he was being used. We would like to think that Matt will marry one day, as we would hate for him to be on his own. But his wife will have to understand him and bear with him.

- You and your partner can be a good example to a teenager embarking on relationships. Let them see you being considerate of each other's feelings, compromising with what the other wants and so on. Explain the give and take of a relationship to them. This is just as important as the facts of life.

Drink and drugs

We did worry about all this, as Matt is not someone who would naturally say no. We had a drink and drug counsellor around to explain the topic to Matt so he understood a bit more and used to tell his friends about the evil effects of drugs or how many units there are in a pint, but that would not stop him from drinking. Over time this calmed down, so I think I was right not to worry too much.

If you have concerns in this area, you can ask the special needs teacher to refer your child to counselling. This is for everyone but they will generally take account of special needs in what they do.

You can find information on drink and drugs on the internet or at the library and talk it through with your child.

Leaving school and thinking about the future

Matt was a pretty normal teenager in that he couldn't wait to leave school and start his college apprenticeship in building. Building needs an understanding of shapes and structures and a love of order, ideally suited to some aspects of Matt's personality. Matt went on to do an NVQ in bricklaying and is now qualified in this. They had helpers at the college for him and it helped him that his dad is in the building trade.

> ## College by Matt Brealy, 24
> *'I found this pretty easy as I had worked with Dad a lot from the age of 14. I clicked with everyone who did the course alongside me. I was glad I did it and it helped me in the long run and I have something I can always do in life.'*

NVQ – National Vocational Qualification – courses at college can be an excellent next step for some ASD children. They will be learning something practical and getting a trade, moving forward. For Matt the problem was to keep him focused on a job. He needed short-term targets and a lot of supervision. We were lucky that we could help to push him towards a job that is tailor-made for his condition. Parents need to find the positives when looking for a job for an ASD person. For instance, many people with an ASD can concentrate on one thing for a very long time, so they can become very good at something they like doing.

- Colleges will help with finding the right course. You could start with your special needs teacher, who should be able to put you in touch with the appropriate people at college.
- Of course, for the more academically gifted ASD children, university will beckon, as it does for most bright children. It is very important that you help your child as much as possible at this stage, with guidance from school or college, to find a sympathetic environment. They need to be comfortable with their choice, able to cope with their surroundings and to be protected from becoming isolated in their studies.
- Some universities and colleges are definitely more receptive to those with additional needs than others, and it is very important to check out this aspect at open days.
- See what extra help the college will supply for them. It can make a huge difference if you find somewhere that is receptive to special needs.

As ASD children get older you may find that it is hard to get the help you need – there is a real gap in provision for teenagers and beyond. We need courses to help parents battle through the teenage years. Once again this pinpoints how important it is to get the statement. Disability allowance can be so useful for young adults. Later our ASD children could be on their own and there is not enough support for them as so many respite-type places are shutting down. We knew that once Matt reached a certain age nothing more could be provided for him. He wants to experience life – we have to keep him safe. It is up to us to put in place what we can to safeguard his future, and this responsibility continues for all parents like us.

Work experience

If they start a college course that will help provide a bridge into the outside world, ASD teenagers are still going to need someone to fight their corner for them. 'I'm always completely upfront with work placement providers,' says Mary Thomason, who arranges work experience for students, many of whom have ASDs, at a centre for foundation studies in the West Country, 'especially because students with even severe autism can look pretty normal. Potential employers have to be aware that there can be problems. For instance, students like this won't want people in their space, like things to run the way they should and can't cope easily with changes. One student can't get to his placement on the bus because he says that if someone sat next to him who smelled really bad, he just couldn't bear it. ASD senses can be so acute that things like that are really dreadful for them. The same boy, who is on work experience at a garden centre, can't cope with getting his hands dirty, so we have made sure that the employer understands that he needs to wear gloves all the time. You have to get placements that are sympathetic to their needs, and this is something that parents should bear in mind if they are not getting the back up from their child's college.'

Mary highlights the importance of getting your child's condition recognised while they are still at school. 'Children whose special needs are not recognised often fall through the net and can be really let down by the mainstream school system. Typically a child who finds things hard to grasp at school will find that teachers don't have time to explain and will probably end up mucking around in class and not get anywhere.'

This vicious circle is the problem with not getting diagnosed, and the many parents who go into denial about their child's condition are really not doing them any favours at all. 'They come to us with issues of communications skills and low self-esteem. We do our best to build them up and from our foundation studies course we can refer them on to mainstream college and courses like plumbing or motor vehicles. Some programmes can propel them in the direction of future employment with things like catering courses in a fully operational cafe where they can learn to take orders, operate the till, prepare food and wait on tables in a working environment.'

Useful organisations

- Foundation for People with Learning Disabilities gives information on issues that affect learning-disabled people's lives, including education and employment: www.learningdisabilities.org.uk.
- Online careers information for young people can be accessed at www2.cxdirect.com.

The answer to a parent's question 'What can my child do next?' has to be that there is no real safety net out there to catch these young people when they get to the end of college. They need ongoing support when it comes to going out to work, and this is only patchily available around the country.

For older teenagers and young adults, computers can be great for their job applications. They can often express themselves better online.

Children with ASD become adults with ASD, but their lives can be made much less challenging with appropriate education and support. While there are some things that will never be easy for Matt, there is not necessarily any limit on what he could do.

Some youngsters will find it hard to move on, but do have a real think about what they are good at, and what they enjoy doing. That may give you some ideas as to their next move. Your child may surprise you as much as Matt has surprised us.

Asperger's advantages by Matt Brealy, 24

'I find it easier to understand people from different paths of life and to relate to young people with problems because I know what they are going through. There are definitely advantages to having grown up with Asperger's.'

17

Young adults – into the future

Bringing up Matt has certainly been a roller-coaster ride for us, but that means lots of ups as well as downs. As a family we are very proud to see how Matt has grown into a happy, outgoing, loveable young man. We will never stop guiding him through his life and I am sure Matt will never stop teaching us!

Growing up by Matt Brealy, 24

'I don't feel I have Asperger's problems any more. There are good things about an ASD frame of mind. With music the concentration and focus can help. For instance, I picked up guitar in a couple of weeks and I play piano and I have got into mixing, which is all about getting two beats together and putting them as one. That just came naturally to me.

'In some ways actually Asperger's seems like an advantage to me now: you just say things; you don't beat around the bush. Eden, my girlfriend, knows exactly where we stand. It is what it is. It makes your emotional life much easier because there are no lies or deceptions. As for future plans, I know I can live independently. I'm not too bad at organisation, and Eden helps.'

Matt's girlfriend, Eden, says that his Asperger's is something she wouldn't have been aware of if he had not mentioned it to her.

'We were on our second date and I mentioned that my little brother was autistic. Matt said he was too, and I was really amazed, as I would never have noticed. But once he had told me there were a few little things that made sense. Matt has a really big personality; that is part of him, but whether it is because he is autistic or not I don't know. A lot of people don't recognise it – and if he hadn't told me, I don't think I would ever have known.'

Benefits of ASD in the workplace

The belief that some aspects of an ASD can confer advantages may be hard won, over time, for parents, but Kate confirms some of the positives in Jack's life. He has found a passion for graphic design and is applying to university while working part-time in a graphic design firm.

'Jack's Asperger's means that he is a very good employee. He works right through the day – he says that he sits down to start work and the next thing he knows, the day is finished and he has worked right through. It is probably a good thing that he is really interested in what he does because that just wouldn't work on the things he is not interested in, but when he is he has the most amazing focus and attention span.

'The ASD mindset has benefits – but it leads to problems too. Jack has a certain amount of trouble with his art and design foundation course – they are trying to encourage the students to "think outside the box", but Jack doesn't really have a box in the first place, so it is frustrating for him.'

One wonderful thing that is just starting to happen is that people with autism are being actively sought out by employers for the positives that can be a feature of the condition. Most notably, Microsoft, the software company has launched a pioneering scheme to hire people with autism in the US, as they 'bring strengths that we need at Microsoft. Each individual is different – some have amazing ability to retain information, think at a level of detail and depth or excel in math or code. It's a talent pool that we want to bring to Microsoft.' This is welcome news: the National Autistic Society estimates that currently only about 15 per cent of adults with autism in the UK are in full-time employment, although a majority would like to be. We can only hope that this recognition of untapped potential will spread to the UK.

Matt now

When he was little, at nursery, it was torture for him to have to be on a stage for the plays they did. He hated to make eye contact or have any sort of confrontation. Now Matt will get up and DJ in front of thousands of people and he is a very sociable guy. However, he is a bit unusual; as he says, 'I don't think there are a lot of autistic DJs.'

Some young autistic adults do need and benefit from sheltered living – it is a broad spectrum of needs, after all. Often, sadly, when they are in homes or in care there is no one to help them with the day-to-day stuff they find hard. When Matt is stuck with forms and other things, he can always get his sister Zoe to help him.

Finding help by Matt Brealy, 24

'That's where it goes wrong for the ones that get put in care – they are on a downward spiral and no one is exactly giving them a good example or helping them. They need help to get a suitable occupation – they are not exactly likely to pick up a book. If they could get onto some voluntary work scheme at least their minds would be active.'

With Matt there is hardly anything you would notice now. He is very literal, say, in dealing with the bank or other bureaucracy. Things like reading paperwork can still be a real problem for him – even though he has left so many of his autistic traits behind. The thing is to be aware of the possible danger areas that continue to lurk for your child, and, as a parent, be ready to step in and help.

Keith is very proud of his son and everything he has achieved against the odds.

'Matty has turned into a friendly young man and mixes with all sorts of people. He is confident and has made a lot of friends because of his forward manner, as he still does not worry about what he says to people and they seem to love him for it as they get a straight answer from him when asked something.

'He still finds it difficult to maintain finances and we keep a close eye on him, so that we can help him to be organised.

'I am proud of what Matty has achieved. He has grown into a strong young man who knows his limitations but does not let that hold him back. I think, through our training when he was younger, he is prepared to try different things knowing that they will make him a better person. He has a lot of friends and is a very loveable person. I feel he should be able to deal with life's problems as he managed to cope well with the death of his brother Paul; he was really strong for all of us and stepped up to the mark when he was needed. He coped well when we went and saw Paul at the morgue and stated that in his view Paul's body was just a carrier for his spirit, and that he thought, and still thinks, that Paul's spirit is still with us. He was actually brave enough to get up at the funeral and do a reading for Paul, which made us all very proud of him.

'I hope he continues to experiment with life and carries on growing into the loving man he has become.'

Now Matt is working as a painter and decorator, and loves his work. His concentration and attention to detail got him the job, and you could say that these autistic traits are standing him in good stead now.

Some youngsters will find it hard to move on, but do look to see what they are good at, and they will probably tell you what they like. Your child may surprise you as much as Matt has surprised us.

Matt has a lot of insight into the condition and because of my work, and the book, he has had to think about it more than he might otherwise have done.

Now by Matt Brealy, 24

'Maybe I am a more thoughtful person because I have had to think about myself and about how things work for me. I have a tattoo that says "Your thoughts and your feelings create your life" – it is out of a book called The Secret, *which is about positive thinking and is a good way of looking at life. A lot has changed since I was 14, when my mum wrote the first book.*

'I think I would be more into studying now than I was then because my goals are clearer. If my schooldays had come later in my life when I had the Asperger's a bit under control, I would have found it a lot easier to study. Things like spelling and writing still get me down.

'I know I am lucky that I enjoy work and making my own money – save, travel, save, travel – you get more insight into life. I have been to loads of countries – Vietnam was the best. The people there are awesome – really happy. We did loads of things there. We helped to rebuild a woman's house. We were travelling and bought some Coca-Colas from the woman and it turned out she had been widowed in the terrible typhoon they had recently suffered and she was pregnant with twins and her house had been really damaged. We weren't doing anything in particular that day so me and my mate helped her rebuild the side of her house even though the other guys working there didn't speak any English and we didn't speak any Vietnamese. Then we ended up leaving her 4.5 million dong (1 million is £30) which was a fair bit for her. Things like that stay in your memories – and if I hadn't been able to get over the problems in my younger life, I would never have been able to travel under my own steam.'

If Matt hadn't learned ways of accommodating his Asperger's into normal life, he would have been at a disadvantage. We stopped Matt rocking and shaking because we knew it made him conspicuous and that mattered because if he was doing it in the classroom it would stop him fitting in with the children he wanted to be friends with. Children can be cruel and I couldn't bear the thought of him suffering the taunts of 'weirdo, weirdo' and then the others walking away. I really felt that if he was an ordinary person doing something like tapping then people would get to know him, because he is basically sociable. And that is what happened.

My future by Matt Brealy, 24

'I want to travel more and see more of the world. I definitely see family in my future and I think I will be a good dad. I would like to have one biological child and adopt one with special needs.'

We were given a very bleak picture of Matt's future when he was diagnosed. I knew I was always going to fight it, and do everything I could to improve the picture – and when you look at Matt now, and see how positive and outgoing he is, with so many plans for the future, and so much ability to make them come true, then it is clear that it was worthwhile.

If you train children from an early enough age and put enough into it so that it all comes together then, if you are lucky, this is what you can have – a child that has a life and a future and a shining light at the end of the tunnel.

To all parents of ASD children, we wish you luck on your own roller-coaster ride.

Useful contacts

National Autistic Society: www.autism.org.uk (helpline: 0808 800 4104)

Ambitious about Autism, a national charity for children and young people with autism: www.ambitiousaboutautism.org.uk

Early intervention

CHAT test details can be found on the National Autistic Society website www.autism.org.uk or on the Child Autism UK website – details below

The Elizabeth Newson Centre in Nottingham for specialist diagnostic early assessment: www.autismeastmidlands.org.uk (01623 490879)

PECS – further information from Pyramid Educational Consultants UK Ltd: www.pecs-unitedkingdom.com (01273 609555)

Child Autism UK (formerly known as Peach): www.childautism.org.uk (helpline: 01344 882248)

EarlyBird Centre (01226 779218): details on www.autism.org.uk

Home-Start: www.home-start.org.uk

National Portage Association: www.portage.org.uk

Hanen: www.hanen.org

Makaton: www.makaton.org (01276 606760)

SenseToys: www.sensetoys.com (0345 257 0849)

Education

Contact a Family: www.cafamily.org.uk (helpline: 0808 808 3555)

Education Otherwise: www.educationotherwise.net (helpline: 0845 478 6345)

Parents for Inclusion: www.parentsforinclusion.org

Advisory Centre for Education (ACE): www.ace-ed.org.uk (helpline: 0300 0115 142)

Bullying and cyberbullying: www.bullying.co.uk

Assessment and benefits

Department for Education (DfE) Publications: www.gov.uk

IASS (Information, Advice and Support Services): www.iassnetwork.org.uk

IPSEA (Independent Parental Special Education Advice), an organisation defending children's right to special education provision: www.ipsea.org.uk

Mencap: www.mencap.org.uk

Disability Living Allowance – find out more at www.gov.uk/help-for-disabled-child

A guide to claiming DLA for children with brain disorders including ASD is available from www.cerebra.org.uk

Disability Rights UK – information and services developed by and for disabled people; includes fact sheets on benefits and how to apply for them: www.disabilityrightsuk.org

Therapies

www.researchautism.net gives impartial advice on therapies

Osteopathic Centre for Children: www.occ.uk.com (020 8875 5290)

British Acupuncture Council: www.acupuncture.org.uk (020 8735 0400)

British Dietetic Association: www.bda.uk.com

British Association for Music Therapy: www.bamt.org

Nordoff Robbins: www.nordoff-robbins.org.uk

Sensory integration therapy: www.sensoryintegration.org.uk

Auditory Integration Training: www.auditoryintegrationtraining.co.uk

Help for teenagers

TEACCH: details of the programme in this country from www.autismuk.com

Foundation for People with Learning Disabilities gives information on issues that affect learning-disabled people's lives, including education and employment: www.learningdisabilities.org.uk

Online careers information for young people at www2.cxdirect.com

The Autism Show takes place each year in London, Birmingham and Manchester: www.autismshow.co.uk

About the National Autistic Society

Around 700,000 people are affected by autism in the UK alone – more than one in 100 – and this figure rises to 2.7 million when you include parents, carers and siblings whose lives can be turned upside down as a result of living with autism.

The National Autistic Society (NAS) is the UK's leading charity for people with autism and their families and carers. Founded in 1962, the NAS spearheads national and international initiatives and provides a strong voice for all people with autism. The NAS provides a wide range of services helping people with autism and Asperger syndrome to live their lives with as much independence as possible, and supporting their families and carers.

The NAS runs a number of schools, colleges and adult services offering day and residential care for people with autism, as well as a supported employment consultancy called Prospects. The NAS also provides a range of support services for parents and families living with autism, from befriending schemes and social groups, to specific programmes and training schemes for different issues affecting those living with autism.

The NAS helpline (0808 800 4104) is a free, confidential telephone support service. For more information about autism and NAS services or to offer support, please visit www.autism.org.uk.

Faces for the fridge

You can cut out or copy these faces and turn them into fridge magnets.

When your child is too emotional to express their feelings in words, they can point to the face that indicates the way they feel, just as Jackie used to do with Matt (see p16).

Happy **Cool**

Sad **Angry**

Worried